POLICY STUDIES IN EMPLOYMENT AND WELFARE NUMBER 3

General Editors: Sar A. Levitan and Garth L. Mangum

Economic Opportunity in the Ghetto: The Partnership of Government and Business

**Sar A. Levitan
Garth L. Mangum
Robert Taggart III**

The Johns Hopkins Press, Baltimore and London

This study was prepared under a grant from The Ford Foundation.

Contents

Preface

Our large central cities continue to provide economic opportunities for the bulk of their residents and for the majority of the rural immigrants attracted by the prospects of economic betterment. But for a large and perhaps growing number, central city ghettos have become a dead end of despair and frustration. Lacking adequate education and training, or excluded by discrimination, they are prevented from pursuing careers and are frequently barred from many jobs. Or if employment is available, it is tedious, low-paying, and unattractive. Entrepreneurial opportunities are even more limited since most ghetto residents lack know-how and financial support. For many, then, the central city economy, especially in the ghetto, does not provide adequate opportunities for self-support and self-improvement.

The government has mounted a variety of programs to expand economic opportunity for ghetto residents. Through exhortation, coercion, and incentives, it has drawn the business sector into these undertakings. Programs have been launched to open existing central city jobs to ghetto residents, to create new private sector jobs in or near the ghetto, and to promote local ownership of ghetto businesses.

This study is an analysis of these joint government-business

efforts, describing their successes and failures to date and pro-
jecting their potential impact. The problems of central city and
ghetto economies are briefly discussed, and several policy direc-
tions are suggested.

This survey touches only the surface of many important issues,
but it is hoped that the broad-brush approach will shed some light
on the problems and prospects of providing economic opportunities for ghetto residents.

We are indebted to our colleague Charles A. Myers, Chairman of the National Manpower Policy Task Force, for a critical
review of the manuscript. The study was prepared under a grant
from The Ford Foundation to The George Washington University's Center for Manpower Policy Studies. In accordance with
the Foundation's practice, complete responsibility for the preparation of the volume is left to the authors.

SAR A. LEVITAN
GARTH L. MANGUM
ROBERT TAGGART III

Economic Opportunity in the Ghetto:
The Partnership of Government and Business

1

The Partnership of Government and Business

Based on aggregate statistics, it can easily be concluded that the average dweller in our largest central cities "never had it so good." Is the "sickness of our cities" therefore largely psychosomatic? Unfortunately, statistics neither alleviate suffering nor resolve social discontent. And though urban problems are hardly new, existing conditions are considered intolerable by large segments of the public as well as by those who have long suffered in silence. This altered social perception has been forced by the urban riots of recent years, the pronouncements of urbanologists, and the mobilization of ghetto residents and the poor under the civil rights and poverty programs. Whatever the causes, a consensus has emerged that something must be done to improve economic conditions in our large central cities.

The economic problems of the central city have many dimensions; their causes are complex and largely intractable. In almost all cases, however, the ills are concentrated in certain areas and particularly affect specific groups—the ghettos and their residents, mostly Negroes.

The conditions in black ghettos are the most visible and per-

1

haps the most severe manifestations of economic stagnation in the central cities. They have been festering for some time, representing neglect rather than abrupt deterioration. And though perhaps not as critical as the riots or the rhetoric of militants might suggest, the problems must be faced. Amelioration of the conditions in central cities, particularly their black ghettos, ranks high on any list of national priorities.

A Bureau of Labor Statistics survey of depressed core areas in Atlanta, Chicago, Detroit, Houston, Los Angeles, and New York City found that in 1968: (1) 70 percent of the residents were Negro; (2) the unemployment rate was two-and-a-half times the national average; and (3) the median earnings of all workers were only $85 per week. Despite the larger-than-average families and the higher cost of living in these areas, median family income was only $5,400, compared with $8,000 for the nation. These conditions are probably duplicated in other central city ghettos.[1]

The booming national economy of recent years has only slightly improved the deplorable ghetto conditions. Moreover, evidence indicates that the ghettos will be the first to feel any slowdown in the economy: recessions in the past have caused an absolute as well as relative deterioration of conditions in these areas.

Federal programs must focus on permanent expansion of the quantity and quality of employment opportunities. As the Kerner Commission emphasized, a twofold approach is demanded which will: (1) improve the access of disadvantaged ghetto residents to existing jobs by breaking down discrimination barriers and by upgrading skills, and (2) increase the number and quality of jobs through economic development of the ghetto.

Increasing Access to Existing Jobs

Unemployment and low wages in central city areas cannot be explained solely by the exodus of businesses. Wilfred Lewis of the National Planning Association has estimated that fifteen large

[1] U.S. Department of Labor, Bureau of Labor Statistics, "Employment Situation Surveyed in Slum Areas of Six Large Cities," February 20, 1969.

central cities lost more than 195,000 jobs to the suburbs between 1959 and 1965, but that the growth of those industries remaining in the city, plus the addition of entirely new types of employment, have made up for this loss. In almost every industry, including manufacturing, the number of central city jobs per central city resident has increased.[2]

The problem is that the new jobs are held by commuters from suburban rings rather than by central city residents. One explanation is that many low-skilled manufacturing jobs have moved to the suburbs, being replaced by white collar jobs for which the residents of central cities are not qualified. But this does not seem to be a valid argument, since the shift to professional and managerial occupations has been even less pronounced in central cities than in the suburbs. As Wilfred Lewis has suggested, expanding central city industries—retail trade, medical and health services, and state and local governments—tend to have an even greater proportion of low-income and presumably low-skilled jobs than the manufacturing industries.

A more valid explanation of continuing high unemployment in central cities in the face of increases in the number of jobs per resident may lie in the qualitative deterioration of the labor force. The inflow of poorly educated rural Negroes and the exodus of better educated middle class whites and blacks may have resulted in a lower quality labor force in the central city. Such differences, however, are not readily discernible in the statistics measuring years of school completed. Though central city averages in educational attainment are slightly lower than those in the suburban rings, the gap has not widened. Qualitatively, however, education in the central cities and the rural "feeder" areas is markedly inferior to that in suburban rings. The actual achievement levels of ghetto high school graduates are significantly below those of

[2] Wilfred Lewis, Jr., *Urban Growth and Suburbanization of Employment—Some New Data* (1969; mimeographed), p. 17. The fifteen cities are: New York, Chicago, Philadelphia, San Francisco/Oakland, Boston, St. Louis, Washington, Baltimore, Newark, Minneapolis/St. Paul, Paterson, Atlanta, Denver, Portland, and New Orleans.

3

suburban school graduates. It is reasonable to infer, therefore, that the skill level of the resident work force has diminished over the years.

It is also painfully clear that discrimination exists in central city employment. The increasing black populations of ghetto areas are still not given equal employment opportunity, much less the compensatory treatment necessary to overcome past discrimination in education and training. The low quality of the labor force is directly related to the lack of meaningful opportunities for training and advancement.

To raise the number of job-holding central city residents, efforts must be made to upgrade their education and skill level to make them more competitive with suburban residents. At the same time, artificial barriers to employment and advancement must be removed, and additional jobs can be developed—preferably concentrating ownership of new enterprises in the hands of ghetto residents.

The strategy of core-city economic development rests on the assumption that the exodus of blue collar and low-skilled jobs to the suburbs, especially manufacturing jobs, can be reversed. While changing production technology (such as the use of single story plants), changing transportation patterns, and demographic dispersion have made centralized location less important and have hastened the exit of plants from central cities, there are indications that these changes have run their course and that technological factors may now be pushing in the direction of greater centralization. Computer technology, for example, has opened a large number of unskilled jobs in "paper-processing." Advances in communications and computer usage permit centralized offices for widely decentralized operations. Increasingly, manufacturing operations require little space, producing instruments or complex products which rely on brain power more than raw materials. Finally, service and health industries, as well as economic activity concerned with urban environmental problems, are becoming more important and are more likely to locate in central cities.[3]

[3] Eli Ginzberg, *Manpower Strategy for the Metropolis* (New York: Columbia University Press, 1960), pp. 59–61.

4

Whatever the balance of technological factors, improvements in the business environment of central cities might be achieved through a wide variety of incentives designed to attract businesses. Such efforts will directly increase employment as well as stimulate jobs in related businesses.

Business Ownership

By increasing the access of ghetto residents to central city jobs, and by developing new employment opportunities in the central city and the ghetto, unemployment can be reduced and earnings and median income can be raised. Though few would disagree that increased income is a necessary ingredient in alleviating the economic and social problems of black ghetto residents, it has been increasingly recognized that control over wealth and capital ownership is also desirable if central city residents are to achieve an equal position in our society. Not only will profits from ownership enhance income, but ownership itself can provide a significant measure of control over one's destiny. Central city Negroes now lack an adequate stake in our economic system. Their sense of frustration is capsulated in the slogan made popular in Harlem several years ago: "There was full employment on the plantation, too!" Most observers of ghetto problems, including the Kerner Commission, have therefore emphasized the need for increased business ownership among blacks along with more and better jobs.

A disproportionately small number of Negroes own their businesses. In urban areas with populations of over 50,000, blacks own 5 percent of all businesses though they comprise a quarter of the population. In the ghettos, they make up roughly three-fourths of the population but own less than a fourth of all businesses, and these businesses are characteristically marginal. A third of all minority-owned businesses are single proprietorships with no employees, and an equal proportion have less than $10,-000 per year in gross receipts. Only 7 percent have more than ten employees.[4] There are only a handful of larger black-owned

[4] Small Business Administration, "Distribution of Minority-Owned Business" (May 19, 1969; mimeographed).

businesses, and few of these are located in ghetto areas. If the Negro residents of the ghetto are to move toward economic equality, they must be given ownership as well as employment opportunities, both inside and outside the ghetto.

THE ROLE OF THE GOVERNMENT

The federal government has assumed an ever increasing role in central city affairs because state governments have tended to ignore central city needs and because city governments have lacked the resources to solve their problems alone. Relying largely on property and sales taxes, city revenues have not grown proportionately with central city income; the tax base has been eroded by the exodus of the middle class to the suburbs; and the costs of and demands for services have vastly multiplied. To a large extent, then, the increased role of the federal government in urban problems has developed by default.

Social and economic conditions in the ghettos have been highly publicized, and the riots have seared the public conscience and convinced legislators that something must be done. Surprisingly, recognition of ghetto problems has occurred at the same time that the political clout of the central city voters 'has been diminishing. In 1952, 41 percent of the total Illinois vote was cast in Chicago and 19 percent in its suburbs; in 1968 the city and its suburbs each accounted for 30 percent of the vote. A similar shift to suburbia has occurred in other metropolitan areas.[5] Nonetheless, many suburbanites commute to jobs in the central city, and the health of the metropolis depends on the well-being of its urban core. Whether from self-interest or from altruistic concern, public tolerance of ghetto conditions has worn thin, and urban problems have become an increasing federal concern. The federal government has undertaken a variety of efforts to solve these problems, playing an important role in hiring and training the dis-

[5] A. James Reichley, "The States Hold the Keys to the Cities," *Fortune,* June 1969, p. 135.

advantaged, as well as in supporting more limited efforts in economic development and the promotion of black entrepreneurship.

The federal government is the largest single employer in the United States. While accurate statistics are not available, it is estimated that the federal government employs about 125,000 central city residents. Despite the impressive numbers, the Civil Service Commission has done little to facilitate the upgrading of low-skilled workers. And, as an employer, the government has demonstrated an even more tenacious concern with credentials than most other employers.[6]

The government has nonetheless initiated programs to provide employment for the disadvantaged, with emphasis placed on the needs of the unemployed for income, work experience, and training. These programs include institutional as well as on-the-job training. The effort began with the Area Redevelopment Act (ARA) of 1961, was expanded with the Manpower Development and Training Act (MDTA) of 1962, and now includes the Job Corps, vocational education skill centers, and vocational rehabilitation centers directed primarily to the disadvantaged. It is estimated that 345,000 persons were enrolled in institutional training programs in fiscal 1969 at a cost of $680 million.[7]

The government has also used its statutory and administrative powers to increase employment opportunities in the private sector by reducing discrimination. The Civil Rights Act of 1964 established the Equal Employment Opportunity Commission, which is charged with investigating and eliminating employment discrimination. In fact the Commission has been given few powers, though during the first four years the Justice Department instituted 6,650 suits against alleged violators of the Act. The Commission's efforts at conciliation have been only partially effective because of its limited powers. Of more practical significance is Executive

[6] Garth L. Mangum and Lowell M. Glenn, *Employing the Disadvantaged in the Federal Service* (Policy Paper No. 13; Ann Arbor, Mich.: The Institute of Labor and Industrial Relations, University of Michigan, 1969).

[7] U.S. Bureau of the Budget, *Special Analysis Fiscal 1970* (Washington: Government Printing Office, 1969), p. 137.

Order 11246, which prohibits employment discrimination by federal contractors. Because the affected businesses employ an estimated 24 million persons, there is a large potential impact, and the order contains stiff sanctions against violators—including contract termination and "black-listing." However, no contracts have yet been cancelled because of charges of discrimination, and it is difficult to measure the indirect effects of the order.

Economic development programs of the federal government have been largely directed to rural areas and smaller cities. However, experimental efforts have been funded in several cities by the Office of Economic Opportunity (OEO) and the Economic Development Administration (EDA), and the Model Cities program anticipates a more comprehensive attack on urban problems. Past programs have had many objectives, but one common purpose has been to attract businesses. The government has offered direct incentives in the form of low-interest business loans and subsidies to improve the infrastructure of areas with high chronic unemployment and to make these areas more attractive to new businesses. Two government programs are specifically designed to assist in the development of industrial parks: the Small Business Administration's (SBA) development loan program can provide up to $350,000 per project, and the Economic Development Administration can make grants and loans for public works to economically depressed areas (though few central cities have received any aid). Economic development on a larger scale requires not only more attractive direct incentives to businesses, but also greater combined efforts by government and business.

The federal government has only recently undertaken efforts to increase minority ownership of businesses. In the past, it was assumed that competition in the free market guaranteed opportunity for the entrepreneur, whatever his race. But discrimination against Negroes in securing credit and the difficulties of black businessmen in breaking into national markets clearly indicate discrimination in the business sector, and most critically among financial institutions. Businesses are traditionally built with other people's money, and Negroes have not had equal access to these sources of capital.

The first steps toward providing capital for minority entrepreneurs, along with some measure of management assistance, were taken with the initiation of the Economic Opportunity Loan (EOL) program under the Economic Opportunity Act of 1964. Administered by the Small Business Administration, this program offered loans and loan guarantees to the economically disadvantaged, with minorities receiving roughly a third of all loans. But the EOL program forms only a small portion of SBA activities: of $623 million in loans made by SBA in fiscal 1968, the EOL program accounted for only $32 million. Within the SBA and Congress, moreover, there has been resistance to making soft loans, and in some cases to making any loans to Negroes. Further, federal lending is miniscule in comparison with private sources: outstanding SBA loans account for less than 2 percent of business loans made by commercial banks. Thus, programs relying only upon direct federal government loans can have only a limited impact. And until 1968, the EOL program was unable to tap the resources of private financial institutions; only six banks participated in Economic Opportunity Loans to minorities. As a result, its impact was limited to direct loans made by the government agency.

BUSINESS JOINS THE BATTLE

The response of the business sector to urban economic needs has varied in form and urgency. Some businesses and businessmen have played an active and innovative role, while others have shunned responsibility. Some efforts have been carefully conceived, executed, and evaluated; others have been nominal or stopgap measures with little hard analysis. The response of the business sector has been far from comprehensive or uniform.

It is hardly surprising, then, that opinions differ considerably as to the contribution of the business sector in solving urban problems. The more sanguine observers, who would agree with Kenneth Clark that "business and industry are our last hope," see in the response a significant departure from past business practice:

"The leaders of American business have been trying valiantly to go beyond the mere rhetoric of social commitment—to really 'do something' about the snarl of problems that have come to be called the urban crisis. . . . On an impressively wide scale, corporations, banks, and insurance companies have taken on obligations that only a few years ago would have been considered quite outside their proper role."[8] Other observers, however, have concluded that the contribution of the business sector has been, on the whole, insignificant: "Business's active involvement in these activities is, as a proportion of the business population, so microscopic as to be almost invisible. Headlines have whipped a thimbleful of soap into a hogshead of lather."[9]

One explanation for these divergent assessments is that businessmen's involvement in "urban problem-solving" is very recent and has thus far borne little fruit. The Public Affairs Council, a trade organization of corporate public relations men, while candidly recognizing the gap between the immensity of the problem and the level of corporate commitment, insists that "a significant beginning had been made."[10]

Another reason for the conflicting appraisals is the difficulty of separating response actions from normal and traditional business practices. As indicated at the outset, the urban crisis represents more a recognition of long-standing problems than any abrupt deterioration of conditions. Similarly, much of the "business response" consists of long-standing practices that have been assigned a new importance. The auto industry, for example, has been hiring workers for many years who meet the current criteria of "disadvantaged." Though such hirings have increased in response to social needs, a large proportion of the disadvantaged would have been employed in the normal course of business. And action has been a response rather than an initiation. The automo-

[8] Allen T. Demaree, "Business Picks Up the Urban Challenge," *Fortune*, April 1969, p. 103.

[9] Theodore Levitt, "Why Business Always Loses," *Harvard Business Review*, March–April 1968, p. 83.

[10] Public Affairs Council, *Corporation and Community Newsletter*, July 25, 1969, p. 1.

tive companies have failed to use their great power despite the commitment of their corporate executives. While business spokesmen repeatedly assert that a meaningful attack on these urban problems requires increased effort and involvement on the part of the business sector, there is no way to measure the total impact of business commitment or to distinguish between commitment and tokenism. No criteria have been devised to distinguish between what the business sector does naturally and what special efforts it has made above and beyond normal operations. This is especially relevant in a tight labor market, because hiring and training the disadvantaged as a result of labor shortages does not imply a commitment to solving social problems. Easing of labor shortages will provide the acid test of the extent of business commitment.

Certain business activities nonetheless are of obvious benefit to the disadvantaged of urban areas. Whatever the motivating forces for such activities, and whatever the degree to which they represent an increased determination to solve urban problems, their aggregate impact can be massive. Intensification of these activities cannot help but improve conditions in central cities.

The most important and basic contribution of the business sector lies in hiring and training the disadvantaged, an activity that can range from providing equal opportunity to intensive efforts to employ the least employable. The most comprehensive efforts include outreach, lowered hiring standards, sensitivity training for supervisors, job counseling and orientation, vestibule or on-the-job training, basic education, and a variety of special services such as health care, transportation, and day care for children. The scale of such efforts is difficult to aggregate, but one dramatic estimate suggested that the operating subsidiaries of American Telephone and Telegraph alone have trained more hard-core unemployed than the Job Corps program.[11]

A second activity of the business sector is the encouragement

[11] Theodore L. Cross, *Black Capitalism: Strategy for Business in the Ghetto* (New York: Atheneum Publishers, 1969), p. 229.

11

of black enterprises. For one thing, management assistance is often provided on a voluntary basis by businessmen and businesses. Franchises, in particular, provide management assistance on a large scale, with the largest two franchisers having more personnel providing technical assistance to entrepreneurs than the total field staff of the Small Business Administration. Larger corporations can subcontract to black-owned businesses, as in the case of General Motor's contract for glove-compartment components from the Watts Manufacturing Company. Similarly, they can deposit funds in black-owned banks: the Chrysler Corporation, for instance, has agreed to deposit $100,000 each month in three black-owned banks. In addition, financial institutions can increase the flow of funds into the ghetto. The First Pennsylvania Banking and Trust Company of Philadelphia, for example, has made more than $1 million in loans to black businessmen in 1968 and has promised more than $5 million. Many banks have created special staffs to promote minority business financing.

The business activity which has attracted greatest attention is the location of branch plants in the central city and in the ghetto. This tactic not only provides jobs for ghetto residents, but through its interrelationship with other ghetto industries, it improves the central city economy.

All these activities tend to raise costs and lower profits. Training costs money, and the investment can be lost to the firm if the worker leaves. Labor costs among the disadvantaged can be high because of absenteeism and turnover. Ghetto businesses are extremely risky, and it is expensive to administer the generally small loans to minority entrepreneurs. Costs of land acquisition, insurance, and construction are demonstrably higher for central city locations. Why, then, should the business sector undertake these costly efforts?

Evidence indicates that prevailing business attitudes have been changing. The urban riots, in particular, are usually credited with motivating a sudden transformation of businessmen's conceptions of their social responsibilities. This explanation conjures up the image of the president and chairman of General Motors atop their headquarters building in a burning Detroit reaching an apocalyptic realization of the seriousness of urban problems and the responsibility of business to help solve them.

Though the riots unquestionably accelerated business activities to help the central cities, the social orientation of the business sector, and especially of the largest corporations and their executives, has been intensifying for some years. Firms have found it necessary to demonstrate corporate commitment to social problems in order to recruit potential top-flight management from the colleges, and as these younger executives increase in number and influence, this "liberalization" becomes self-sustaining. Likewise, public opinion concerning the role of business in solving social problems has gradually shifted. A 1968 public opinion survey by the Opinion Research Corporation found that 60 percent of all those sampled felt that corporations should take an active part in the poverty program; only 19 percent felt they should not. Of even more significance, 65 percent of stockowners favored an increased role for big business. Certainly this atmosphere has had much to do with the total business sector effort, but it offers little explanation for the variety of responses from individual businesses. This variety can only be explained by the differing views of top management concerning the social responsibilities of their corporations.

The bulk of the visible efforts are made by the corporate giants such as AT&T, Avco, IBM, Brown Shoe, General Electric, Prudential, and the Chase Manhattan Bank, although their achievements to date may be more a reflection of effective public relations than solid accomplishments in the ghettos. Among the larger firms, the degree of involvement depends on fairly predictable factors: those which motivate the firm and those which determine how much the higher costs will affect profits.

One source of motivation is the firm's direct ties to the central city. Firms having large facilities in the central city, or doing a large portion of their business there, can be expected to exhibit more concern over urban unrest than firms lacking these characteristics. Utilities, for instance, have a large capital investment in

13

ghetto areas; large department stores are dependent on the stability of the city; insurance companies have concentrated their facilities in central cities; and downtown banks are often restricted by law from moving outside the city. These categories of firms have thus been in the vanguard of efforts to hire and train the disadvantaged, to develop entrepreneurs from minority groups, and to improve the economy of the ghetto.

Government persuasion and coercion may also be an effective motivator. Defense contractors have played an important role in improving employment opportunities. Some of the most active corporations have been involved in antitrust action and may be conscious of the need to improve their public image. Though these firms have rarely been subject to overt coercion, it is clear that one purpose of their good works is to purchase favor.

A third determinant is the degree to which the costs of good works can be passed on. Utilities with public guarantees of profit and many defense contractors with provisions for compensating the higher costs of buying from minority-owned firms or hiring the disadvantaged provide cases in point. Such tight oligopolies as the automobile industry can also pass on the costs, since all of the big three are carrying on similar programs and incurring similar costs. Firms in less-concentrated industries may act as cartels. The insurance industry, for example, pledged $1 billion in loan funds on a pro rata share to attack urban blight. To the extent that size insulates a firm from price competition, larger firms are also more likely to become involved in social problems.

Meaningful corporate commitment depends, not surprisingly, upon the degree to which urban problems affect the business, the extent to which demonstrated effort helps managerial recruitment or assures government markets, and the proportion of costs that can be passed on. Though the attitudes of businessmen may have changed, their actions as corporate executives still depend, for the most part, on their calculation of the best interests of their businesses in the traditional sense.

14

NEEDED: JOINT EFFORTS

Conceptually, it is possible to separate efforts by the business sector and those made by the federal government to improve the ghetto and central city economies. This distinction has proven useful in identifying the motivations and inherent limitations of such multilateral efforts.

The business community has assumed a continually expanding social responsibility. It has undertaken programs for hiring and training the disadvantaged of central cities. Several large firms have opened ghetto branch plants that have increased the number of jobs for ghetto residents. Entrepreneurship has been promoted through market guarantees by large firms, while banks and other lending institutions have in many cases made special allowances to increase the number of minority loans. These actions, however commendable, have hardly made a dent in the problems of the ghetto and are unlikely to intensify to any meaningful degree. It is trite but true that businesses operate for profits, and business resources cannot be committed on a large scale without the promise of profits. Cursory analysis has shown that most of the achievements so far have been by firms seriously threatened by ghetto problems, those which are insulated from the costs of social commitment, or those which stand to benefit from such activities. Despite the rhetoric, traditional rules of the game have changed little.

The government is also limited in what it can do. Its resources for promoting entrepreneurship are small in relation to similar resources in the private sector which might be tapped for the same purposes. Nor is there evidence that society is willing to grant sufficient priority to allocate the vast resources needed for an all-out attack on ghetto problems. Though the government is a large employer, its manpower requirements are dwarfed by those of the private sector; and except for special-purpose programs, it is governed by much the same motivations for efficiency that tend to exclude the disadvantaged elsewhere. In promoting economic development, the government can open new facilities in the ghetto or can try to improve infrastructure so that businesses will be attracted, but the costs are massive and experience with the Area Redevelopment Act and the Economic Development Administration would suggest that such an indirect approach is ineffectual. With the present level of funding, the government can promote annually a few thousand minority businesses. But without management assistance from the business sector and acceptance of ghetto products into national markets, these firms will remain marginal regardless of the scale of federal funding.

To point out the limitations of these efforts is merely to slay a paper dragon; it has long been recognized by both sectors that urban problems require a partnership between government and business. In practice, government programs have been aimed at encouraging the utilization of private resources and tapping the reservoir of social commitment found in the business community. This partnership aims at increasing access to jobs and developing the ghetto economy through attracting businesses and promoting minority entrepreneurship.

2

Private Involvement in Manpower Programs

Federal outlays for manpower programs have increased tenfold during the 1960s. The increase in expenditures has been accompanied by changes in the goals and emphases of federally supported manpower programs. A major shift has been the intensified effort of private employers to help train and employ the poorly educated and unskilled. Federal appropriations for manpower programs administered by the Department of Labor amounted to $1.4 billion in fiscal 1969, with one of every six dollars allocated to private employers. As proposed by the administration, the private employers' share in fiscal 1970 would double out of an increased budget of $1.6 billion.

The increasingly active role of private firms began for reasons of publicity and profit, continued because it had budgeting advantages, and finally became the preferred practice because it seemed to be an effective way to guarantee jobs to disadvantaged participants. Because the channeling of manpower and antipoverty funds from public agencies to private firms has been substantial, and because the public-private partnership has profound significance for the economy and society, it is imperative to understand the experience and implications of these programs.

17

TRENDS IN PRIVATE INVOLVEMENT

Private employer involvement in manpower programs for the disadvantaged has been most evident since President Johnson's manpower message of January 1968, when he announced the formation of Job Opportunities in the Business Sector (JOBS), a major effort to induce greater private participation in manpower programs. Actually, however, there were a number of precedents. From its beginning, the Job Corps contracted with private business firms to operate centers—a decision made because of the mystique of business efficiency and the expected favorable reaction of Congress and the public.

On a broader age scale, the Manpower Development and Training program encompassed both institutional and on-the-job training (OJT), with the latter rising from 6 percent to 48 percent of the total effort between 1963 and 1968. Simple economies encouraged this shift in light of the fact that the MDT budget remained relatively stable over the years. By avoiding stipend and equipment costs, OJT could enroll three trainees for the price of one institutional trainee, a consideration that strongly favored OJT. Also persuasive was the fact that, once enrolled, the OJT worker had a job, while the institutional completer still had to be placed. To overcome the difficulties of placing disadvantaged persons in OJT "slots," the Labor Department sought assistance from subsidiaries of private firms specializing in training, hoping that employers would be more responsive to entreaties from corporate officials than to appeals by government bureaucrats; but the efforts were without success. The Concentrated Employment Program (CEP) also began with an objective of providing brief orientation courses for the disadvantaged and then placing them with private employers. The failure of these experiments forced the government to raise the level of subsidies to employers to induce them to hire the disadvantaged. By the summer of 1967, following riots in various cities, the emphasis was upon offering "instant jobs."

On the other hand, training programs had worked well for resi-

18

dents of suburbs and small cities who lived near where the jobs were located. But such programs proved frustrating for ghetto residents who too often ended their participation with only a "hunting license" to seek jobs which remained illusive for reasons of location or discrimination. If only employers had determined to "hire now and train later," ghetto residents would have believed their message. To be sure, prevocational training is presumably necessary even for entry-level unskilled and semiskilled jobs. But, it was reasoned, the training might be more acceptable if offered at the work site and on the payroll. To induce employers to change their hiring practices and to offer "guaranteed jobs," the government stood ready to pick up the tab.

THE ORIGIN OF NAB-JOBS

Following several experiments to induce firms to locate in ghettos, the Labor Department in December 1967 invited some 700 companies in five cities to bid on contracts to "hire first and train later." The requirements were stringent, but the government promised to pay all the extra costs. Enrollees were to be hired immediately; basic education, training, and supportive services were to be provided after hiring. In order to qualify, each contractor had to promise at least fifty jobs and submit to standard reporting, monitoring, and financial controls. Employers were to receive a fixed negotiated price per trainee for a fixed period of time, after which, if the employee had been retained, an incentive bonus could be paid. Though seventy-five firms indicated interest and eighteen Manpower Administration (MA) contracts were signed, the potential of this approach was never tested because the program was replaced by new efforts.[1]

Some businessmen complained that the stringent controls and monitoring contemplated by the Labor Department would alienate the business community and discourage their cooperation. Accordingly, in his January 1968 manpower message, President

---

[1] Known as MA-2 contracts, following upon the MA-1 contracts which had attempted to use private firms as OJT promoters.

Johnson announced the Job Opportunities in the Business Sector (JOBS) program to be promoted by a National Alliance of Businessmen (NAB), chaired by Henry Ford II. Prodded by a national NAB office staff directed by another Ford Motor Company executive on leave, local NAB offices in the fifty largest cities, staffed with local business executives on loan from their companies, contacted private employers in search of signed pledges to hire the disadvantaged. The goal was 500,000 jobs by June 1971. Within the limits of its budget, the Department of Labor was prepared to pay the added costs of hiring, training, and retaining low productivity workers through a series of new (MA-3) contracts. No additional funds were requested from Congress, but appropriations from existing manpower budgets were reallocated to support the initial goal of filling 100,000 jobs by June 30, 1969.

NAB appealed directly to the employers' conventional values. JOBS was not pictured as another "do-good" program or even as riot insurance. Rather, the business community would profit in a number of ways. Less unemployment would mean better, safer cities in which firms could function; it would provide ghetto residents with money which would in turn generate increased consumption; welfare and kindred expenditures would decrease, thus indirectly affecting company taxes and perhaps reducing governmental involvement. In addition, the tight labor market was stressed as an incentive to enlarge the effective work force. In brief, the program constituted an appeal for businessmen to help themselves by helping others.

The business response surprised all but the most optimistic. Forty percent of those contacted, primarily major firms, pledged to hire disadvantaged workers. The initial assignment of finding 200,000 unsubsidized youth jobs for the summer of 1968 was not fulfilled, but 165,000 permanent jobs were pledged within six months in contrast to the goal of 100,000 by the end of one year. By July 1, 1969, no less than 338,000 jobs had been pledged. Some skeptics predicted that the best that could be expected of private employers was that, for a large enough subsidy, they would put the disadvantaged on their payrolls and provide needed polishing afterward. To the surprise of many observers, two-thirds of the initial pledges were from "volunteer employers," or so-called "freebies" (pledges to hire the disadvantaged without application for government reimbursement).

The ease of obtaining the pledges, it soon became apparent, had created a false sense of euphoria. Getting pledges was one thing, but turning them into job orders and then into placements was another. Pledging employers had not been asked to specify the date of the intended hiring or the rates of pay and qualifications of applicants. Employment service representatives who called upon pledging employers found that some intended to fill the positions through their own recruiting efforts, or promised to do so at some time in the future. Others claimed they had already made good on their pledges but offered no evidence.

On the other hand, some public employment service agencies and CEP administrators were unable to fill NAB's job orders because their outreach efforts were inadequate or because they were not trusted by members of the poverty community. Many of the jobs offered had already been listed at employment services. By the fall of 1968, job openings equaled less than one-third of the pledges, and placements were less than one-half of the openings. Employers were claiming two-thirds as many additional gate hires as had been placed through the official agencies. Placements under MA-3 contracts were only one-eighth the number promised in outstanding contracts.

As soon as the deficiencies became obvious, the business executives assigned by their companies to run the national and fifty local NAB offices began pressuring their employer constituents, while the Labor Department remonstrated with the employment services. Each sought better relations with the other. Convincing employers to work through the CEPs was even more difficult, and most of the fifty local NAB "metro" directors were at a loss to determine who among the many self-proclaimed ghetto leaders were the appropriate community contacts. Like earlier manpower programs, JOBS could progress only by an experimental, trial-and-error process. One of the most important lessons of its initial

21

period was to count success in terms of people placed rather than jobs pledged. The realization that retention and upgrading were even more important soon followed from additional experience.

NAB-JOBS IN PRACTICE

To qualify for government reimbursement, employers in the NAB-JOBS program must hire workers meeting the standard Labor Department definition of "disadvantaged." The hired employee must be poor and either unemployed or underemployed, as well as one of the following: (1) under twenty-two or over forty-five years of age; (2) a minority group member; (3) less than high school graduate; or (4) handicapped. Because many NAB participants resented the implication that this was "another Negro program," the minority aspects of the program were minimized in the public statements issued by NAB. Nonetheless, most workers hired under the program were black. A new euphemism was created: hired employees were "subject to special obstacles to employment." The "volunteer employers" confronted no legal requirement, and many of these employers appeared to consider black and disadvantaged to be synonymous.

The actual characteristics of enrollees in NAB-JOBS programs are summarized in Table 1. The limited data upon which the table was based suggest that enrollees under MA contracts are more likely to be nonwhite and encumbered with other employment handicaps than "freebie" enrollees. This probably reflects continued "creaming" in the unsubsidized hiring process. Despite the presumed creaming, the discharge rate is higher for "freebies," perhaps indicating that without reimbursement employers are less willing to put up with absenteeism, tardiness, drunkenness, and other problems of ghetto clientele.

The fact that most of the noncontract enrollees are employer-certified leaves the credibility of the noncontract aspect of the NAB-JOBS program in doubt. The requirement that a state employment service or CEP certify that employees hired under Labor Department contracts conform to the criteria of "disadvantaged"

Table 1. Characteristics of NAB-JOBS employees, cumulative April 30, 1969[a]

Characteristics	Total	Percents or Averages	
		Contract	Noncontract
Male	75	71	77
Negro	73	78	70
Handicapped	1	1	1
Age average	27	27	27
Under 22	40	43	39
45 and over	8	8	8
Family size average	3.6	3.7	3.6
Annual family income	$2,628	$2,474	$2,767
Years of education	10.5	10.3	10.6
Weeks unemployed last year	21	23.0	20
Certified by			
Employer	46	2	68
Employment Service	37	72	20
CAA/CEP	12	22	7
Other	5	3	5
Termination			
Quit	48	49	48
Discharge	37	36	38
Layoff	5	4	5
Other	10	12	9

[a] These data based on 63,700 hiring cards referred by April 30, 1969, and represent 48 percent of total hiring claimed by that date.
SOURCE: U.S. Department of Labor.

lends those figures more weight, though some complain that anyone "with a black face and a torn shirt" can be certified. There has been no check of the validity of the claims of noncontract employers. Though they had little incentive for false reporting, the low percentages of reporting leave ample room for bias in the data. Considering the tight labor markets of 1968–69 as well as the locations of many of the firms involved, it is difficult to know whether the proportion of disadvantaged among noncontract hires exceeds that which would have occurred without the program. The differing characteristics of noncontract and contract employees does, however, indicate that the latter incentive affected hiring practices.

23

It is extremely difficult to determine what training is provided workers hired under MA contracts, and it is impossible to do so for more than a scattering of employers engaged in hiring "freebies." Determining costs for contracting purposes was a matter of negotiation—based on the employers' estimates as restrained by the Labor Department's notions of an appropriate per capita ceiling.

Under the plan, employers were to be reimbursed in equal monthly (usually twelve) installments, which were to cease if the employee quit or was fired and was not replaced by another disadvantaged worker. Any initial capital investment or starting costs that exceeded the average monthly costs would have to be recouped by the company during later months, creating "front-end loading" with a built-in incentive for retaining workers for the full contract period. To date there has been little auditing or follow-up to determine how much training and other promised services have been provided, and what has been the resulting employment and earnings experience of the placed employees. Only three sources of information are available, all less than satisfactory: (1) analysis of contracts in force, indicating the intentions of contract employers; (2) a survey conducted for the Urban Coalition in the fall and summer of 1968 that provided data on the practices of 224 firms involved in the NAB-JOBS effort;[2] and (3) personal observations and interviews at the national and regional level and in eight of the original fifty NAB cities.

Contractual Obligations

Almost all MA-3 contracts called for orientation and basic education. However, only a third contemplated more than the standard company orientation concerning product lines, work and safety rules, pay scales, and fringe benefits. Three-quarters promised basic education averaging 160 hours. Counseling was

[2] E. F. Shelley & Company, Inc., *Private Industry and the Disadvantaged,* prepared for the Urban Coalition (New York: 1969).

24

promised in two-thirds of those contracts analyzed, with job coaching in four out of five—though confusion obviously existed over the meaning of these two services. Some form of health care was included in four of five contracts, but only one out of five provided for more than pre-employment exams and minor corrective treatment. Three of five contracts promised transportation assistance, though most apparently intended to arrange car pools. MA-3 contracts reflected more generous funding and consistently provided more diversified services than MA-2 contracts.

Of most interest is the fact that only one-fifth of the MA-3 contracts contemplated pre-job training and only one-fourth promised skill training and aptitude testing. Considering the entry-level nature of the jobs, the lack of any information concerning the extent of on-the-job training and the apparent absence of planning for advancement raise doubts concerning the quality and durability of the jobs provided. Apparently basic education, counseling, health care, and job coaching were expected to bring the new employee to competitive status with other employees; sensitivity training was expected to remove negative elements from the supervisor's attitude; and transportation assistance was assumed necessary to bridge the gap between ghetto residences and job locations. Beyond that, with few exceptions, the disadvantaged employee was apparently to be treated like every other. In other words, contractual indications of intent suggest a pattern departing only modestly from customary practices.

More than four of five MA-3 contracts had some type of hiring restriction. Two-thirds of them were related to physical ability, probably reflecting the preponderance of semi-skilled manufacturing jobs. One-fifth had educational requirements; one in eight included emotional strictures and the same proportion required various special skills.

Half the promised MA-3 jobs provided a starting rate between $1.60 and $1.99 per hour, with more than a third from $2.00 to $2.49 and one in eight above $2.50. Following the initial training period, the wage rate of over one-third of the jobs was to be between $1.60 and $2.25 per hour, a similar proportion between

$2.26 and $3.00, and one-fourth between $3.01 and $4.00. As might be expected, the promised wage rates varied geographically according to prevailing wage patterns.

An analysis of the contracts throws little light on the proposed relationship between federal subsidies and job content or pay. Payments differed widely for jobs with similar titles promising, for instance, subsidies ranging from $1,000 to $3,600 for janitors and $2,000 to $3,900 for laborers. One company was to receive $3,700 for employing and training a clerk while another firm in the same city contracted to prepare punch press operators at $2,500 apiece. In another city, $3,400 was the incentive to one company for employing office boys, compared to $1,800 for material handlers. Waitress jobs in one contract came at $3,000 per employee. These wide variations in reimbursement reflect lack of data about training costs and the bargaining efforts of the cooperating employer. Government representatives, under pressure to get proposals in and contracts signed, were not in a position to haggle over prices. Since the services to be provided can be expanded or contracted to fit any prescribed ceiling, no solid base for pricing exists.

Two-thirds of the MA-3 job slots were promised by firms with over 2,000 employees even though only 28 percent of the contracts were with firms of that size. Over 90 percent of the MA-3 contracts were with individual firms; only eighteen contracts involved more than one firm.

Employer Practices

The study sponsored by the Urban Coalition set out to examine the practices, rather than the promises, of 224 large firms in twenty-nine industrial classifications engaged in 298 separate projects. Nearly a third of the projects had received federal funding or expected to do so. The study was limited in that only fifty of the company programs (including sixteen funded by the government) had been in operation over six months, 128 for less than that, and 46 were still in the planning stages.

Every firm with an active program reported altering its normal screening procedures and standards to favor NAB recruits. Aptitude testing had been generally dropped or qualifying scores lowered, though some firms retained tests to determine needed remediation rather than to screen out applicants. Cultural biases in customary testing techniques were widely conceded.

The advent of tight labor markets had apparently reduced the high school diploma as a prerequisite for employment and was reflected in the contracts; growing recognition of the uncertain quality of a ghetto school diploma reinforced that trend. White collar firms, however, seemed reluctant to lower education and literacy requirements.

Four of every five firms had altered previous standards regarding criminal records, though most firms continued to disqualify applicants for convictions involving arson and sexual or narcotics offenses. Many firms had ceased automatically disqualifying those with records of violent felonies; two had even hired convicted murderers. Bonding requirements had also been relaxed, though they still tended to block those with theft records from jobs where temptation was prevalent. Most companies also bent their rules against hiring employees with garnishment and indebtedness records.

Physical disability was the largest single cause of rejection, and few companies attempted to help remedy such defects. Most of those who did offer help merely referred the applicant to a public health service. The most common change in screening procedures was relaxation of past work histories, which were replaced by the interviewer's assessment of worker attitude.

One-third of the companies treated their hard-core employees, once hired, no differently from any others. Six of every ten reported that they gave no special consideration to former trainees once the training period was completed. Yet the thirty-eight firms able to compare turnover of the new employees with that of regular employees produced surprising results. In the automobile and other industries that had long hired large numbers of low-skilled minority workers, the application of the "hard-core" definition to recruits had no significant effect on turnover. The higher reten-

27

tion rate of the more formalized government-funded programs was impressive. However, only 4 percent of all the firms reported any special efforts to upgrade the disadvantaged into better jobs. The most frequent reasons given for not doing so were seniority problems and the hostility of regular employees.

More than 80 percent of the respondent firms had launched some type of internal training to prepare supervisory personnel for dealing with disadvantaged employees. Only 40 percent, however, provided some type of sensitivity or attitudinal training, with the remainder relying merely upon a brief discussion of goals. Less than half aimed the training at management personnel.

AN APPRAISAL OF NAB-JOBS

Eighteen months of experience with NAB-JOBS is hardly an adequate time span for definite assessment of its contributions. As a program launched by administrative decision within existing authority and reallocated budgets, however, it is absorbing scarce funds that might have been used in other ways for the same objectives. In particular, JOBS grew at the expense of institutional skill training and public service employment (Table 2). The 1970 Johnson budget recommended further expansion of JOBS, and the Nixon budget continued that emphasis, apparently in part at the expense of the Neighborhood Youth Corps (NYC) and the Job Corps. The obvious question is whether the shift in funds has been justified.

As with any public program, the key to evaluating the NAB-JOBS effort is to distinguish between the rhetoric of the sponsors and reality. As we have seen, early public relations treatments confused easy-to-get pledges with hard-to-accomplish job placements. Once the wide margin between pledges and placements became apparent, both NAB and Labor Department officials, to their credit, shifted the emphasis to placements. Yet the question remained, How many more people are now hired, and in what ways do those hired differ from others who might have had the jobs? The program will raise total hiring: (1) when the subsidies

28

Table 2. Source of NAB-JOBS funding

(millions)

	Fiscal Year 1968[a]	Fiscal Year 1969	Fiscal Year 1970
Total	$113.8	$159.7	$420.0
Manpower Development and Training Act[b]	41.6	47.9	240.0
Economic Opportunity Act	59.6	111.8	180.0
Economic Development Act	2.8	—	—
Special Impact	9.8	—	—

[a] Test cities, MA-1, MA-2.
[b] Includes some Fiscal Year 1967 funding.
SOURCE: U.S. Department of Labor.

are attractive enough to make worthwhile expansion of production; or (2) when the newly recognized availability of labor leads to filling vacancies which would otherwise have gone unfilled; or (3) when social conscience induces employers to forego profits or exploit opportunities they would have otherwise ignored. In most cases the employers themselves probably do not know when one or more of these conditions have been fulfilled, but a significant net addition to the total number of jobs seems highly unlikely. Granting that the program does not create jobs, the extent to which it redistributes them might be judged by comparing the characteristics of the new NAB-JOBS employees with nonprogram employees. Since no such data exist, the answer to the latter part of the above question must remain a matter of speculation.

The Uncertain Record

NAB claimed a total of 230,000 job placements through August 1969. Fifty-four percent of those hired were still on the job, though the meaning of a gross retention measure that lumps those still employed after more than a year with those hired only the day before is uncertain. Cohort data on the number enrolled at a point in time who are still employed at a subsequent date several months later have not been complied or supplied. But in evaluating the NAB-JOBS retention rate, the typically high

29

turnover in low-skilled entry-level jobs must be kept in mind. Only 55 percent of the total labor force works full-time all year, and many of these undoubtedly change jobs in the process.

The validity and significance of the numbers claimed is by no means clear. Of the 230,000 claimed placements, only a fourth were in jobs covered by federal contracts, while the rest were "freebies." In about one-fourth of the cases, "hire cards" were submitted by employers listing the demographic characteristics of the workers. JOBS had no information about the rest, except that their hiring was apparently reported orally to NAB metro directors with no other details given. Termination cards are also expected from employers in order to calculate the retention rate, but there is little incentive for such reporting from the noncontract employers.

As an example of the uncertainties in the reporting system, one city credited with having substantially exceeded its quota reported 2,800 hires in fulfillment of 3,300 pledges, though 800 were followed by terminations. Upon checking, it was disclosed that the company with less than 2,000 employees had pledged to hire 1,500 "freebies" and reported retaining 1,300. Fewer than 100 hire cards were sent in by the company. The firm experienced a strike during the period, and one wonders whether it counted the employees recalled when work was resumed as hired replacements, or whether it experienced extremely high turnover.

Without contractual obligation or payment, however, nothing is lost except the credibility of NAB if some reported hires are unfounded. Any additional hiring of the disadvantaged by these firms is a bonus.

Where the reported hires are confirmed, the question remains whether JOBS and NAB changed the hiring practices of the reporting companies. For instance, it was reported that Negroes at the Ford Motor Company rose from 12.3 percent of the total employees in 1962 to 17.5 percent six years later; at Chrysler the comparable figures were 12.6 percent and 23.8 percent; at General Motors 8.1 percent and 11.6 percent.[3] With trends of

[3] "Business and Race," *Wall Street Journal,* June 11, 1968.

this nature established prior to the existence of NAB-JOBS, the extent to which subsequent hirings of blacks in tight labor markets were affected by JOBS is a matter of speculation. Ford, for instance, hired approximately 3,000 disadvantaged workers between October 1967 and April 1968—mostly before the NAB efforts were initiated. The major change in traditional practices was the location of recruiting offices in the ghetto. General Motors, though accounting for over one-fifth of all national NAB-JOBS hires during the first year, claimed no special efforts or special privileges for their reportedly disadvantaged employees.

To separate the effects of an early blossoming of social consciousness from those of a tightening labor market and the company's consistent needs for unskilled workers is to attempt to unscramble the proverbial egg. The NAB director for the Detroit area claimed that if the city were given another pledge of 20,000, it would be unable to fill the jobs, especially since two of every three unemployed are women and most manufacturing jobs are restricted by law or practice to men. Obviously, the automobile companies had nowhere to turn but to the disadvantaged.

Information on hiring activities by employers under JOBS contracts is more dependable, though it is not without problems. The government reimburses employers for hiring a specific individual and ceases payments when the individual leaves or the contract expires. No checks are made to ascertain that the claimed hires are actually on the job—though it is doubtful that the firms would risk fraud for the amounts of money involved. Each contract hire is certified by the public employment service or the CEP to be a bona fide disadvantaged person. Inaccuracies might result from normal operational weaknesses but are unlikely to reflect collusion.

In the tight labor market that prevailed during the first year of NAB, many firms had exhausted other sources of supply and turned to poorly educated persons from minority groups. Yet prodding from the NAB-JOBS effort may still have been the key to tapping this unfamiliar labor pool.

The experience of the auto industry again provides an example. Negroes hired under Ford's inner-city recruiting program dif-

31

fered from previously hired "walk-ins" (black or white) in that the ghetto hires tended to have been unemployed for a longer period of time. They performed just as well on the job and even proved a little more stable than the average assembly-line work force. Nonetheless, the automobile companies apparently altered hiring practices in some cases. In addition to its broader effort at ghetto recruiting, Ford initiated an experimental four- to fourteen-week vestibule training course for 250 seriously disadvantaged people. Under a $1,170,000 MA-3 contract, the company set a goal of hiring sixty-five illiterate relief recipients (forty women and 25 men), ninety male NYC dropouts, seventy released prisoners, and twenty-five NAB hires who had quit their jobs. Chrysler put more than 1,200 workers through vestibule training under a $13.8 million contract, and nearly a fifth of these were illiterate.

Financial and other traditionally white collar industries, accustomed to hiring from "mainstream" populations, had less successful experience. The new hires differed considerably from the accustomed work force of the firms not only in dress, language, and color, but also in work attitudes which exhibited themselves in higher than normal absenteeism and tardiness. However, these firms accounted for only a small proportion of total NAB hiring.

After all the available data and studies have been examined, and after national, regional, and local interviews have produced conflicting information, it must be admitted that the basic questions remain unanswered. Many employers have undoubtedly made significant contributions to the welfare of disadvantaged workers and their families, but no one can say how much difference the program has made.

Variations in Performance

The speed with which national NAB officials, all on temporary loan from their jobs in industry, sold the program to the business community and got it underway was impressive. Their evangelistic fervor gained solid support from Labor Department officials and staff who carried the actual burden of administration, negotiation, and support at the national, regional, and local levels. However, exclusive reliance upon executives loaned by cooperating companies restricts, if not completely precludes, Negro participants in NAB, because few of the corporate executives are black. NAB's inability to provide adequate technical assistance to aid participating employers in the unfamiliar task of assimilating the disadvantaged, as well as the unsettling effects of constant turnover among local NAB volunteers, have led some within NAB to advocate permanent staffing. Yet this would create a private bureaucracy which would soon be guilty of most of the ills which beset the public counterpart.

NAB's effectiveness differs widely by region and city, depending upon the enthusiasm, competence, and policies of the local chairman, metro director, and those who work with them, as well as upon labor market conditions. Reported hires and retentions as a percentage of target varied widely by region and by city, ranging from 1.5 percent to 430 percent of quota. The variation may have had as much to do with the realism of the target as with the amount of effort. Visibility, political activity, and availability are likely to influence the selection of the chairman, who in turn normally appoints the metro director. In some cities, firms loaned their best men and in others their hacks. Initially, some metro directors showed a proclivity for seeking out the most militant community leaders in the target areas and avoiding CEP, the community action agencies, and the employment service. The uncertainty of who represented whom soon became apparent, and the local NAB offices' reactions varied from seeking out stable institutions and groups to participate in the program to ignoring them and "going it alone" with individual companies or consortiums doing their own outreach, recruitment, and screening. The notoriety occasioned by the Boston "shoot out" among minority leaders, all in pursuit of MA-3 funds, was followed by a firm alliance between NAB and CEP in that city.

As with most new voluntary organizations, local NAB efforts varied in effectiveness according to the ability, interest, and re-

33

sources of the chairman and executive director. In some cities the programs never came to life because of an inactive chairman; in other places, the level of activity changed with the turnover of on-loan personnel. In one west coast city, NAB leaders decided to concentrate on securing pledges, leaving employers to decide whether they would seek the supporting contracts. The result was many pledges but few contracts. It is next to impossible to tell how many of the pledges were actually filled or the extent to which those hired differed from those already on the payroll. In contrast, a new director took over a moribund organization in an eastern city. Suspecting the "freebies," he concentrated on securing and administering MA contracts, forcing changes in those he considered inefficient. Pledges in that city are fewer but results are more apparent and testable. However, the director's rapport with the disadvantaged community is now much better than his relations with the business community.

In another west coast city where there is no dominant firm or industry, one especially socially conscious company sparked the formation of a consortium by underwriting it financially. It offered to advance, where necessary, the funds to support the front-end loading and promised to reimburse any firm that experienced losses under an MA-3 contract. The consortium established its own school and recruited its own enrollees, largely ignoring the local CEP and employment service, though the latter was obliged to certify the enrollees before participating employers could qualify for government reimbursement. Despite the hard-core certification, most enrollees at the school were walk-ins and their performance there and on the job suggested that they were not the most disadvantaged and certainly not the least motivated. Nevertheless, the consortium's training facility does a competent job of pre-employment training, places the trainees in appropriate job slots (in the process violating the "jobs first-train later" philosophy), follows them with job coaching or even reprocessing through the training facility, and places them with another employer if the first job fails to work out. Yet, despite the consortium's success, employers in the city were reluctant to seek contracts; at least one participating employer admitted that "I only pledged a few jobs to NAB to get all of those job developers off my back."

In every city the proportion of participating firms is low. In one, the Chamber of Commerce assumed special responsibility for promoting the program, but only 125 employers—out of 7,000, including 3,000 Chamber of Commerce members—made pledges. As in most cases, the cooperating employers tended to be either the largest or most visible—public utilities and banks, for instance. Consumer-oriented firms tended to be the most vigorous in "talking up" their involvement. Forty-five firms accounted for a third of the money obligated under the 1,050 MA contracts during the first eighteen months of the JOBS program.

Some Labor Department contracts have gone to firms established specifically for the purpose of training. Other firms have emerged to provide technical assistance or other services. Dozens of firms, old and new, are providing sensitivity training of undetermined value to the reported 5,000 supervisors receiving it. In one city it was reported that the most significant representation in behalf of MA-4 contracts was from such firms anxious for business as subcontractors. But, though subject to abuse, these are all legitimate entrepreneurial functions. One training firm was refused an MA-3 contract to train auto mechanics when it failed to gain the support of the black community. An individual entrepreneur sought to take over the program, gaining supposed community support by forming a consortium of new firms, each headed by a militant black leader and each assigned some piece of the total training action. The financial losses which occurred when some individuals landed in jail fell not on the taxpayers but on a parent firm which had assumed the costs of the front-end load for the new organization.

Yet for every anecdote of a firm on the make or less than fully committed, there are equally documented cases of firms going far beyond their contractual obligations to absorb extraordinary costs and expand extra efforts. One of many such examples is Western Electric's establishment of a feeder plant in a Newark ghetto that offers basic education and on-the-job experience until

35

the enrollees meet the standard qualifications for employment and can be transferred to regular plants in the area.

Unions, Wages, and Long-Run Effects

Though the AFL-CIO has been less than enthusiastic about subsidizing private employers, it is providing support through a Labor Department contract of its own. A few national unions have been strong supporters though most remain neutral. Local union involvement in company efforts to hire the disadvantaged seems to be limited and characterized by watchful waiting of the leadership and latent and sometimes open hostility among the rank and file. Negotiations for changes in hiring and probationary rules have been possible as long as seniority remains inviolate. Next to tampering with seniority, the surest provoker of hostility appears to be the discovery that white applicants are being turned away in favor of blacks. Opposition becomes more bitter in the wakes of feared layoffs, as in the aircraft industry, which faces decreasing defense orders. A development, as yet minor, that is disturbing to employers and union leaders alike is the emergence of rump factions of new employees demanding a larger voice in union affairs as well as concessions from management. These have been particularly noticeable in the automobile industry, where the Dodge Revolutionary Union Movement (DRUM) has fomented work stoppages and the League of Revolutionary Black Workers has picketed the headquarters of the United Automobile Workers.[4]

Most of the hires thus far have involved unskilled and semiskilled jobs in manufacturing, particularly in the automobile industry. In contrast, industries, like basic steel, that have higher proportions of skills and definite multirunged skill ladders have made few NAB pledges, though labor shortages have forced lowering of their pre-1966 hiring thresholds. Few jobs have been offered in construction and transportation and there is considerable

[4] Peter Henle, "Some Reflections of Organized Labor and the New Militants," *Monthly Labor Review*, p. 20.

resistance by potential employees to participation by hotels and other low-wage industries. The numbers of participating employers in financial and other white collar industries is small but growing. A critical factor is the state and structure of the labor market. Detroit's excellent record for well-paid blue collar jobs is a product of high demand for semiskilled automobile assembly workers; on the other hand, the city has little to offer unskilled female applicants. In Washington, New York, or San Francisco the reverse is true, and good jobs for males are scarcer than those for females.

A three-way controversy over minimum wage scales raged for some time among employers, the Labor Department, and ghetto leaders. The Department understandably refused to negotiate contracts for jobs paying less than the federal minimum. Employers complain that any prevailing wage is legitimate; whereas ghetto spokesmen—recognized or self-appointed—argue that a job without status and upward mobility is little better than no job at all. In fact, experience has shown a definite pattern of minimum wage rates, differing by city, below which it is difficult to attract JOBS applicants: $1.60 in Dallas and Houston; $1.75 in Atlanta and Portland; $1.80 in Baltimore; $2.00 and above in Boston, Buffalo, Chicago, Los Angeles, Philadelphia, and St. Louis; and $2.50 in Milwaukee and Seattle.

Only careful evaluation—including longitudinal follow-up studies and cross-program comparisons—can determine which route provides the best long-run employment and earnings record. Conceivably, skill training might prepare for better initial jobs; by contrast, the "instant job" has been primarily entry level. In practice, however, few training programs have prepared the disadvantaged for other than entry-level jobs. Employers may also be more patient with their own disadvantaged recruits than with those of similar characteristics and problems who are hired from a training program.

On the clearly positive side, JOBS has stimulated participating firms to re-examine their personnel policies. Though labor shortages undoubtedly lowered educational barriers, NAB-JOBS participation has underscored the questionable relevance of educational credentials to job performance. Police records, once an absolute block to employment in many if not most firms, are more and more applied selectively according to the nature of the crime and the job. Probation periods have been lengthened to increase chances for success, though employers retain the right of firing before seniority rosters are loaded with those gaining permanent rights but having only temporary ambitions.

The tendency for firms to establish community service or urban affairs departments, providing both talent and resources and a built-in interest in continued service, has been accelerated through NAB participation. Some major firms have added information about their social activities to their annual reports. Though many, if not most, firms have been reluctant to trust CEPs and employment services, the net result has been closer relations and probably improved rapport between public agencies and private business. A bonus is a new realization by employers of the high costs associated with remediation and the advantages to the community and economy of better initial preparation for employment.

Companies without training programs or with fragmented ones have been moved to establish coherent and centralized policies. As one employer put it, "I saw that training was good for the disadvantaged new employees and then I realized that all my employees needed it."

One interstate food chain had left all personnel policies to individual store managers. As a result of its participation in an MA-3 contract, the firm established a central hiring policy featuring top management endorsement of minority hiring. Where new employees had previously been fired if they could not "cut it," regional training facilities were established under the new program. New employees were bussed to a central place, given a few weeks of basic education and vestibule training in a simulated retail grocery operation, followed onto the job by coaches, and brought back for periodic refresher courses. Though used so far only with MA-3 enrollees, the company says it intends to make the practice permanent. The cost of the particular contract, more than $5,000 a head, appears excessive in contrast with the training provided, yet the value of the long-run change in the company's personnel practices may be considerable.

THE FUTURE OF NAB-JOBS

The Nixon administration has firmly committed itself to the JOBS program, though its well-publicized LBJ brand may restrict White House enthusiasm. Secretary of Labor George P. Shultz has endorsed the program as well as the fiscal 1970 appropriations of $420 million recommended by his predecessor.

Data Needs

Any judgments about NAB-JOBS must await the development of adequate data. Even though the early tendency to emphasize pledge figures has been overcome, there is some reason to question the credibility and reliability of NAB-published data on hirings and retention rates. While NAB data are mainly compiled by telephone reports from the metro directors, and are only partially substantiated by hire cards, Department of Labor figures are based solely on actual hire and termination cards. Labor Department figures on hirings and on-board trainees have consistently been lower than comparable NAB figures, and the discrepancies cannot be explained by incomplete reporting alone.

There are also no follow-up data on the enrollees after initial NAB placement or information on their occupational training, either on a contract or a noncontract basis. Many conclusions on the need for and success of federal subsidization programs could be drawn if data were available on the size, location, and industrial makeup of the participating companies.

Another aspect of the program that needs study is the relative success of enrollees who have been categorized by certification source. Studies of the NAB program in individual cities suggest that enrollees who are referred by the CEP offices perform somewhat better than those referred either by the state employment service or those hired directly by the participating firm. Possibly some CEP offices, anxious for success, have been more selective than either the employers or the local employment service office. A more likely explanation may lie in the orientation or prevocational training the worker received at the CEP center prior to going to the NAB company. If a widespread correlation could be established between NAB success and orientation, prevocational training, or some other factor, new hiring procedures would be suggested. The fact that the new CEP guidelines call for much closer cooperation between the local CEP and NAB offices, and that any new NAB job openings must first be offered to CEP enrollees, may indicate thinking along these lines.

Available statistics indicate that women account for about one of every four JOBS enrollees, a ratio considerably lower than in related programs. It is not clear whether the high proportion of men is due to successful outreach efforts, reluctance of employers to change hiring practices based on sex, or the fact that semiskilled manufacturing jobs predominate among pledges.

Determinants of Success

The preceding analysis indicates that the faith in JOBS usually stems not from proven performance but from a gut feeling that the program works. The apparent initial success of NAB-JOBS can be attributed to a combination of riot-borne fears, presidential publicity, evangelism on the part of prestigious business leaders, growing sensitivity to human distress, and labor shortages. Though it involves only a small proportion of U.S. employers, its publicity has made social service the "thing to do." Even if fully achieved, however, its objectives will hardly dent the problems of labor market disadvantage. Considering the rapid turnover, 500,-000 persons can be run through entry-level jobs without noticeable effect in the fifty or more metropolitan areas. Nevertheless, the jobs will be vitally important to those helped.

Changes in NAB leadership have occurred at the local level, sometimes for the better and sometimes not. The first "change of the guard" at the national level, from Henry Ford II to Donald M.

Kendall, occurred simultaneously with a new federal administration and is providing a real test of the durability of business evangelism. Indeed, the program almost got lost in the transfer of power. Only the persistence of the Labor Department, whose new leadership was already committed to the approach, and of NAB staff left behind after the departure of the top leadership, finally surfaced it among all the new concerns of an inexperienced White House staff. Having weathered that dangerous passage, the program could shed the stigma of being a Great Society effort.

The crucial threat to the program is its dependence on labor shortages. Aware of this threat to the NAB program, company and government personnel search for measures to offset the last-in first-out proclivities of normal business practices and negotiated labor agreements. The recruiting centers established by Ford Motor Company in the Detroit ghettos have alternately closed and opened, depending upon short-run demands. Substantial numbers of new workers recruited by the automobile companies have experienced layoffs, though many have been employed long enough to earn recall rights. The United Auto Workers and committed management people in the automobile industry hope that, given the income protection provisions of its labor agreement guaranteeing senior employees up to 95 percent of take-home pay for fifty-two weeks, such employees can be encouraged to accept voluntary layoff in deference to the new workers. In light of the high cost involved, most managements are reluctant to accept the burden of paying double wages, one to the junior worker retained and another to the senior on layoff. Because NAB hires differ in no significant way from many others on the payroll, granting such protection for some junior employees may require it for all. Few employers are likely to be able, even if they are willing, to continue employing disadvantaged minority members while senior employees accept the burden of unemployment.

All the elements—riots, presidential publicity, business evangelism, and labor shortages—were necessary to the program's launching. Some may be dispensed with, given current momentum, but it is difficult to believe that the program could continue at meaningful levels in soft labor markets. If this does not destroy the program, it still remains to be seen whether the commitment of the business community can be sustained over the long pull. Lack of enthusiasm appears to plague many of the seventy-five additional cities to which the current administration is seeking to spread the program. The newly launched MA-5 contract series appears to be attracting a cool response, and there is reason for administrative concern that the $420 million proposed for reallocation to JOBS from other programs for fiscal 1970 may be difficult to spend.

Unresolved Issues

Assuming that NAB-JOBS continues, several administrative problems will have to be resolved. The issue of permanent staffing will probably recur. Impatience with the procedures and capabilities of local public agencies will continue, and NAB executives will opt for taking over outreach, recruiting, screening, and other presently public functions. Companies will grow weary of the costs, and individuals will tire of the sidetracking of careers; the temptation will be to seek government funding for permanent staff. If this occurs, it would bring about profound changes in the nature of the program. Bureaucracies are bureaucracies, public or private. The individual accepting a permanent public service post with little opportunity for advancement, even though on a private payroll, is very different from the ambitious business executive on the way up. Thus far NAB executives have been the salesmen, and civil servants the technicians; there is little evidence that either would be good at the other's role.

Whether and in what form the program will continue may be murky. That it should continue is clear. It has worked its way through a "Madison Avenue" stage of fascination with numbers and appears to be settling down to a concern for performance and permanence. The objective is redistribution of existing employment and not generation of new jobs. Smaller firms must be brought into the action; their involvement will require consortiums

42

or public agency-business partnerships, the latter offering the jobs and the former the training and other services small firms cannot provide. They will want their employees "processed" before rather than after they come on the job, but this will not preclude tying a job guarantee into the training program. Incentive provisions are already changing to offset the front-end loading problem. There has been some tendency to move from noncontract to contract relationships, though the growing number involved has kept the contract-noncontract mix from changing significantly. Somewhere along the line firms will have to submit to meaningful evaluation to reassure the taxpayer that he is getting his money's worth. While at NAB's insistence Labor Department officials have tolerated permissive policies—expending federal funds without getting an accounting from employers—Congress and the General Accounting Office may insist on more customary procedures.

The emphasis of the program will continue to shift with experience. Upgrading is being added to the initial activities expressed in the slogan of "hire, train, and retain," and these changes are reflected in contract provisions. MA-3 rewarded placement and retention in entry-level jobs, MA-4 added an optional standard reimbursement rate for placements in middle-level skills, and MA-5 adds an upgrading option. Under the last, a participating firm receiving reimbursement under an existing contract may negotiate for added compensation if it undertakes to upgrade up to 30 percent of the employees hired under the earlier contracts. These are to be primarily employees who have been with the firm for at least twelve months in low-wage, low-skilled jobs and who are unable to rise through normal company procedures. However, up to 30 percent of the total upgraded employees need not be among the disadvantaged, as long as they are trained to work in occupations where "skill shortages" exist.

Despite these adaptations and the commitment of the Nixon administration to JOBS, the number of firms signing contracts on a case-by-case basis is bound to remain small. Separate negotiations and contracts with individual employers or employer associations do not lend themselves to massive enrollments, especially if monitoring is taken seriously. Replacing project-by-project funding with tax incentives could broaden the employer participation; but there is no guarantee that tax incentives will be a reimbursement for hiring the disadvantaged, rather than another tax relief measure for business.

Currently under discussion is a Public Service Careers (PSC) program which offers the same employment subsidies to public agencies. Too often a false dichotomy is made between private and public, or profit and nonprofit employment. In fact, all provide goods or services demanded by consumers and all offer job opportunities at wage rates determined in the labor market. The real distinction is between jobs for which consumers are willing to pay the full cost and jobs which are specially created to employ the disadvantaged. Subsidies for hiring designated individuals serve to reimburse employers for low productivity within their work force, for higher training costs, or perhaps simply for putting aside prejudices. But little is added to total employment. However, most public employment proposals call for the creation of new or additional jobs to perform useful services. When the direct gains accruing to the deprived are added to the societal benefits resulting from reimbursing public agencies for hiring the disadvantaged, the case for expanding public employment can become persuasive.

Subsidized private employment is one more tool in the kit available for helping the competitively disadvantaged find their way into sustained labor market participation. It is no substitute for adequate preparation, nor is it a way to open the door to jobs requiring substantial skills. In the long run, the emphasis should be on improvements in education that would prepare ghetto youth for the good white collar jobs which abound in central cities but which currently remain in the domain of qualified suburbanites.

If the promise of education or training is to be believed by those made cynical by the failure of past commitments, a direct and observable tie to a job guarantee must be involved. Subsidies are a logical approach to helping the disadvantaged compete for entry-level jobs against those who are more fortunately situated. If NAB-JOBS is not structured properly to establish a direct tie between training and employment, it must be made so or another device must be designed. The concept is right and the machinery must be implemented.

3

Attracting Businesses to the Ghetto

The most visible way of improving employment opportunities for ghetto residents is to induce new businesses to locate in the area. Though a traditional panacea for ailing local economies, there has been little agreement about how businesses can best be encouraged. Compared with manpower programs, very little public money has been spent on attracting businesses to central cities. Those communities that have succeeded in luring industry reflect diverse conditions and have offered various subsidies and inducements. Success has often been the product of intangible ingredients. Also, past experience with government incentives has been concentrated in rural communities or smaller cities, and the lessons learned are not necessarily transferable to the large central cities.

No single formula has been devised for attracting businesses to the central city or its ghettos. But four steps are involved in any design to lure new industry: first, priorities must be established for the desired location of the new business—whether it is to be located within the ghetto, near the ghetto, or anywhere in the central city; second, the special problems of doing business in the specified area must be identified; third, industries that will most effectively satisfy the area's needs must be identified; and fourth, adequate incentives must be offered to attract these businesses.

THE TARGET AREA

New jobs must obviously be within commuting distance of the ghetto if they are to have any impact. Preferably, the businesses should be induced to locate within the ghetto itself. Not only will the workers find it easier to commute to ghetto plants, but even more important they will be more apt to take advantage of job opportunities in their own area. Moreover, new enterprises will also have a secondary effect on the ghetto economy by increasing the demand for ghetto goods and services and inducing additional expansion of employment.

At the same time, several factors weigh against business locations in ghettos. Business conditions are usually much more uncertain in ghetto areas, and firms must be given larger inducements to locate there than on the peripheries of established industrial areas. Moreover, most ghettos are chiefly residential rather than industrial or commercial areas. Attempts to develop ghetto land for industrial purposes have often met with resistance from local residents. Furthermore, there are no exact geographical boundaries to the ghetto. For these reasons, it may be more desirable to attract plants outside but near the ghetto. Nevertheless, the accessibility of new jobs to ghetto residents must be a primary consideration.

The work mobility of ghetto dwellers is limited. A survey sponsored by the U.S. Department of Housing and Urban Development (HUD) found that a third of central city families and half of its poor families are without cars.[1] A sampling of disadvantaged workers in Watts found that less than half had access to an automobile, and that a fifth of these cars were unsafe and two-fifths were not insured.

[1] Thomas H. Floyd, "Using Transportation to Alleviate Poverty: A Progress Report on Experiments Under the Urban Mass Transportation Act" (Washington: American Academy of Arts and Sciences, June 8, 1968; mimeographed).

Ghetto residents must rely mainly on public transportation, which in most cities is inadequate because it was designed to deliver workers to and from the central business district rather than to points across it. In south central Los Angeles, HUD found that the average travel time to the heavy industrial concentrations at Santa Monica, Torrance, and Long Beach was an hour and a half, covering a distance of over fourteen miles; the one-way fare averaged $1.00. Clearly few workers are willing to spend three hours a day commuting to low-paying jobs. Conditions vary in different cities, but transportation problems often deter ghetto workers from seeking and holding available jobs within the city. These problems must be considered in determining the location of new business.

There are practical obstacles to specifying target areas for locating new businesses. Earlier area development programs have shown an inherent tendency to spread development resources too thin. Many marginally depressed areas clamor for and receive certification, and Congress as well as federal officials have succumbed to pressures for distributing expenditures evenly within certified areas. This same tendency may be even more acute in the cities, where there are no political boundaries to ghetto areas, and where the poor are found in numerous smaller pockets of poverty as well as in the larger ghettos. Practically, it would be impossible to give subsidies for firms to locate on one side of a street and not to firms on the other side.

Exact specification of target areas is nonetheless as necessary as it is difficult; without it, development funds can be frittered away with little impact. This seems to have been the case with locational grants made by the Department of Labor in fiscal 1968 to eight private firms from antipoverty Special Impact funds.[2] The program was aimed at "particular communities or neighborhoods within those urban areas having especially large concentrations of poor persons." The legislation further specified that "all projects

<hr>

[2] Westinghouse Learning Corporation, *Report on the 1968 Special Impact Programs*, Report to Office of Economic Opportunity (January 30, 1969; mimeographed).

and related facilities will, to the maximum feasible extent, be located in the area served." However, this mandate was not translated into administrative guidelines by the Office of Economic Opportunity or the Labor Department when contracts were negotiated with five firms in Los Angeles and three in New York. Though the target areas were determined, the "maximum feasible extent" to which firms were required to locate in these areas was never specified. As a result, none of the five Los Angeles firms located in the target area; likewise, two of the three New York firms located at a considerable distance from the target area, Bedford-Stuyvesant. The effects on the target areas have thus been minimal despite the expenditure of more than $8 million in subsidizing these firms. If development efforts are to have an impact, hard decisions must be made early in the game in defining boundaries of the target areas and in requiring subsidized enterprises to locate near or within these boundaries.

THE BUSINESS ENVIRONMENT

Most businesses must be offered incentives to locate in or near the ghetto to offset the unattractive business environment. Many factors, monetary and nonmonetary, lead businessmen to prefer locations elsewhere.

Of the economic considerations, perhaps the most significant is the higher cost of labor. This is difficult to quantify because of varying labor mixes, but available data indicate that payroll per employee—including wages and salaries, fringe benefits, and social security—is higher in the larger central cities than in the rest of the nation. In the retail, wholesale, and service industries, it is also higher than in the suburbs of the larger cities. Only in manufacturing is the central city payroll per employee lower than in suburban areas, though it is still higher than the national average (Table 3). Such labor costs are, of course, largely determined by the types of industries located in cities, but they nevertheless affect the prevailing rates which new industries must pay.

Adequate data are not available to compare payroll costs in the

49

Table 3. Comparison of annual payroll per employee in the twenty largest central cities, their suburbs, and nation, 1963

| | Central City as Percent of | |
Industry	Suburbs	Nation
Manufacturing	95	107
Retail	105	105
Wholesale	107	109
Services	102	106

SOURCE: Derived from the Bureau of the Census, *County and City Data Book*, 1967.

ghetto with those elsewhere in the central city. Obviously, low-wage industries would cluster in ghettos to take advantage of the pool of unskilled workers, but there is little to indicate whether concentrated unemployment leads to lower wages for similar industries elsewhere in the city. Statutory minimum wages would tend to reduce wage differentials between ghetto areas and other parts of the central city. On the other hand, unions seem to have little power in the low-wage ghetto industries, having either failed to organize their employees or made special arrangements to allow corporations to bend union work rules and wage scales.

Other factors push labor costs higher in the central cities than in the suburbs, and probably higher than elsewhere in the city. One component is the cost of training workers. Fitting low-skilled workers to low-skilled jobs requires little training. But if meaningful employment opportunities are to be brought to the ghetto through plant locations, someone will have to bear the cost of training the disadvantaged workers.

The costs of training vary with the quality of instruction and counseling, the capability of the trainee, and the type of available jobs. As noted earlier, federal grants to subsidize the differential cost of hiring and training the disadvantaged under the JOBS program averaged $2,800 per trainee. Training the average disadvantaged enrollee under the MDTA-OJT program cost about $650 in fiscal 1968. Another determinant of training costs in

50

Table 4. Program cost per enrollee by funding source

(*percent*)

Cost Range	Company-Funded	Government-Funded
Total	100	100
Under $500	25	5
$500–$999	19	5
$1,000–$1,999	36	17
$2,000–$2,999	8	20
$3,000–$3,999	6	31
$4,000–$4,999	6	12
$5,000 and over	0	10

Source: E. F. Shelley & Company, Inc., *Private Industry and the Disadvantaged Worker*, prepared for the Urban Coalition (New York: 1969), p. 48.

the past has been the source of funding. Not surprisingly, companies have been willing to offer more expensive and hopefully more intensive training programs when they are funded by the government. This is indicated by the survey of training programs prepared for the Urban Coalition (Table 4). Whatever the exact costs of training, they are clearly substantial—especially if the firm is to have real impact on the problems of the disadvantaged ghetto workers, giving them qualitative as well as quantitative opportunities.

Another element of labor costs is losses resulting from high turnover rates. As might be suspected, tenure in all low-wage industries tends to be short. But there is little evidence that firms locating in the ghetto will encounter higher turnover than enterprises paying comparable rates elsewhere. Ghetto residents are more likely to remain at jobs closer to their homes than they are at jobs to which they must commute. The Urban Coalition study found that turnover rates were no greater among the disadvantaged workers than among other workers at the same jobs, and they were often lower where the job opportunities were meaningful (Table 5).

Absenteeism, probably more than turnover, contributes to the high cost of employing disadvantaged workers. The experience of the few large companies opening branch plants in the ghetto

51

Table 5. Labor turnover rates

Rate of Turnover of Disadvantaged Compared to Regular Workers	Total	Company-Funded	Government-Funded
Significantly lower	29	25	40
About the same	50	50	50
Significantly higher	21	25	10

SOURCE: Same as Table 4, p. 73.

has been highly unfavorable in this regard. IBM's Bedford-Stuyvesant plant, which has had no particular trouble with turnover, has reported the rate of absenteeism to be twice that of its other plants. Other companies have experienced even higher relative differentials in absentee rates. Absenteeism, like turnover, is inversely related to the quality of the job opportunity. Even so, a serious problem of the disadvantaged worker is the network of circumstances that influences attendance and work responsibility—conditions that are difficult to alter.

Numerous other economic factors weigh against ghetto locations or, for that matter, locations anywhere in the central city. More than $100 million in property was destroyed in the 1968 riots, and the fears of businessmen cannot be dismissed as overreaction. Tangible evidence of increasing crime, vandalism, looting, and arson has resulted in skyrocketing insurance rates within the central city; some ghetto areas have been red-lined by insurance companies so that no coverage is available at all. Another costly complication of locating businesses in our larger central cities is compliance with complex building codes and related ordinances. IBM estimated that renovation costs for its Bedford-Stuyvesant plant were 10 percent higher than elsewhere in the city.

Undoubtedly one of the most serious obstacles to locating business in the central city is the scarcity and high cost of land. Piecing together the land tracts required by sizable enterprises is difficult because of the numerous owners and complex zoning ordinances. The delays in acquisition and preparation cause firms to choose more readily available sites. But the major ingredient is the higher cost of land in the central city. According to the President's Committee on Urban Housing:

> Within any given metropolitan area, the cost of land tends to rise as one moves toward the center of the city. Land costs in downtown areas, even in slum areas, are extremely high compared to suburban land. Land in urban renewal areas, after clearance, has sold on the average from $158,000 per acre in New York City, and $39,000 per acre in Philadelphia. However, the steepness with which land prices drop off as one travels away from the central city is less pronounced than it used to be.[3]

The high cost of land is one reason why firms prefer suburban locations to those in the central cities, but it does not explain why firms locating in the central city prefer to build outside the ghetto. One reason is that because ghettos are largely residential, it is more difficult to piece together large land tracts. Less than 3 percent of all land in the twenty-five largest cities is used for industrial purposes. Firms find it easier to use the land that remains available, especially when it is developed as an industrial park.[4] Nor has the lower cost of ghetto land in the wake of the riots offered an incentive to new businesses, for the low price is but a reflection of the high risk.

Nonmonetary factors impede location of firms in the central city and especially in the ghetto. Managerial, professional, and skilled white collar workers, with greater mobility and perhaps greater concern with an area's amenities, are increasingly reluctant to hold positions in the largest cities. Higher living costs, the tedium of commuting, crime and violence, and many other problems are associated with central city locations. The "amenities" factor looms large in locational decisions and may contribute to the higher salaries needed to attract managerial, professional, and other skilled workers.

[3] The President's Committee on Urban Housing, *A Decent Home* (Washington: Government Printing Office, 1969), p. 141.

[4] The National Commission on Urban Problems, *Three Land Research Studies* (Report No. 12; Washington: Government Printing Office, 1968), p. 23.

Perhaps the most potent nonmonetary liabilities of ghetto locations are uncertainty and fear. Lacking meaningful data on ghetto business conditions or comprehensive analysis of recent experiences by ghetto enterprises, businessmen must rely on rumors about ghetto economic conditions. And these are the sources of apprehensions, justifiable or not. An intensive nationwide study of ghetto plants by IBM's staff found widely varying conditions among central cities but little data to help in planning for its Bedford-Stuyvesant plant.[5]

The risk and uncertainty surrounding ghetto conditions constitute a serious detriment to the location of new enterprises in these areas. Unless future conditions can be predicted more reasonably, or unless a "risk subsidy" is offered to firms locating in the ghetto, businessmen will understandably remain reluctant to commit corporate resources. To attract plants to the ghetto, inducements must be offered which would make allowance for the uncertainties as well as the hard costs of ghetto operation.

Three Case Studies

A handful of larger corporations have already established branch plants in the ghetto. Their experience, though certainly not definitive, tends to support conclusions drawn from the limited aggregate data. While these ghetto subsidiaries are hardly representative of the varied industries already operating in the ghetto or hiring its residents, their experience will prove decisive in attracting additional firms.

Three of the most highly publicized ghetto efforts are Aerojet-General's Watts Manufacturing Co., EG&G's Roxbury subsidiary, and IBM's plant in Bedford-Stuyvesant. They are fairly typical of the recent ghetto efforts of such other large corporations as Control Data Corporation, Warner-Swazey, Brown Shoe Company, Avco, Fairchild-Hiller, Lockheed Martin-Marietta, Xerox, and Eastman-Kodak.

[5] Edward Banfield, *IBM-Bedford-Stuyvesant Facility*, Conference to Employ the Disadvantaged (Cambridge: Harvard University, January 30, 1969; mimeographed).

The earliest and perhaps the most widely heralded ghetto investment by big business was Aerojet-General's formation of the Watts Manufacturing Company as a wholly owned subsidiary in 1966. The action was clearly prompted by the riots that ravaged Watts the year before. The company was formed in such a hurry that it incorporated and hired a black president and general manager before anyone decided what it would produce. Indeed, lack of forethought and sound business planning has been the major weakness of the Watts effort. The company has had to adapt itself to changing markets rather than fulfill the proven needs of its parent.

However, the Watts Manufacturing Company was launched at a propitious moment, as the Vietnam war created large demands for military supplies and the War on Poverty focused attention on the needs of disadvantaged workers. Soon the company was able to negotiate a $2.5 million contract to supply the Department of Defense with large military tents, backed by a $1,300 per-man training subsidy from the Labor Department. Hiring 500 workers from among the most disadvantaged in Watts and expanding into fourteen buildings, Watts Manufacturing Company soon found itself in the tent business.

The company took a loss on its first tent contract, though this was perhaps to be expected because of start-up difficulties. But problems have continued. Additional smaller contracts have been secured with DOD, but the labor force has been cut back to less than 300 and attempts to diversify have been unsuccessful. The problems are clear-cut. In the first year, 1,200 employees had to be hired to maintain a work force of 500, and the company found that its training costs were closer to $5,000 per man than to the $1,300 provided by the Labor Department. As a result, Aerojet-General has lost several hundred thousand dollars. As one of its executives reportedly summarized the experience, "There was a lot of flag waving in the beginning, but when the hurrahs died down, we were caught in the middle of it."[6]

[6] Allan T. Demaree, "Business Picks Up the Urban Challenge," *Fortune*, April 1969, p. 174.

In March 1968, EG&G, a major nuclear and oceanographic research corporation, opened a metal fabricating subsidiary in the Roxbury ghetto of Boston. This venture was launched with a little more planning than the Watts Manufacturing Company, but as the president of the company commented retrospectively, "I guess we tried to accomplish too much, too fast."[7] EG&G was not only inexperienced in light metal fabrication, but it proceeded to hire a group of disadvantaged workers and four black managers, all of whom were totally unfamiliar with such operations. This subsidiary was given an unusually large degree of autonomy, with the intention of spinning off ownership within twenty years through stock options to employees.

EG&G had little internal demand for fabricated metal products, so outside markets had to be developed. Such markets have not been forthcoming. And the inexperience of the workers and managers has taken its toll as overhead has run about three times wages—where in the normal fabricating operation it amounts to roughly half. Despite a $575,000 training grant from the Labor Department, the plant lost $75,000 in 1968 and anticipated a loss of $250,000 in 1969. EG&G has been forced to reduce its labor force and release two of its four black managers.

Perhaps the most carefully studied and successful ghetto location is IBM's Bedford-Stuyvesant plant. Beginning operation in July 1968, the plant has continued to expand its labor force, with an anticipated complement of 450 employees by the end of 1969. It originally produced computer cables for IBM, but this proved unprofitable. The plant has gradually shifted to producing power supplies, which it has been able to do at less than outside vendor costs (although considerably more than the cost at which IBM produces them in its other plants).

Two major factors account for IBM's success in contrast to EG&G and Aerojet-General's rather dismal experiences. First,

[7] Tim Metz, "EG&G in Roxbury: 'Too Much, Too Fast,'" *Wall Street Journal*, July 3, 1969.

considerably more planning went into the Bedford-Stuyvesant effort. There was less fanfare, with goals consciously being understated to the public. Most significantly, the plant was producing for an internal and guaranteed market: the demand was known and only the question of supply remained to be worked out. Second, entry-level wage rates in the plant were high for the labor market—a minimum of $2.12 per hour plus substantial fringe benefits and job security. As a result, IBM's experience with its labor force has been favorable, with very low turnover and much less absenteeism than at either EG&G or Aerojet.

IBM's experience has dispelled or at least quelled many of the myths about ghetto operation. Crime and vandalism have not been a problem; the work force has shown itself to be productive and responsible; profits have been realized; and all this has been achieved without any government subsidy. However, IBM has not been free of problems, and it has been uncommonly lucky in avoiding others. For instance, it encountered high costs—including occupancy, sales taxes, and building costs—that are endemic to operating within New York City. Fortuitously, it acquired a lease on an unoccupied building at less than half the prevailing rate; few, if any, locations of this size remain within Bedford-Stuyvesant. Other firms locating in this or other ghetto areas have not enjoyed such favorable experience with land acquisition.

Other subsidiaries and firms provided with a guaranteed (and often noncompetitive) market have duplicated IBM's modest success. Examples are a printing plant launched in Boston by Avco to do its own internal printing and a Xerox-FIGHTON partnership in a Rochester metal stripping plant to produce for the parent company. Without this critical factor of a guaranteed market, ghetto plants and subsidiaries have generally had disappointing performances. Some of these recent corporate efforts have undoubtedly suffered from hasty implementation or birth pains, and may prove more profitable in the future. But if these plants do not get out of the red soon, some will probably be abandoned and further ghetto locations will be discouraged as a consequence.

The Types of Industries

The particular firms and industries to be placed in a given city must be chosen on a pragmatic, case-by-case basis. But a few general guidelines should be applied to limit the initial possibilities. A number of theoretical considerations should also be resolved, or at least be confronted explicitly, prior to the selection of specific industries or firms.

Quite obviously, the preferred industries will be those least affected by the problems and costs of ghetto or central city operation—thus requiring fewer inducements to locate there—and those offering the greatest probable impact on ghetto residents. Often there must be a trade-off between the two characteristics, for the industries most easily attracted are not necessarily those most needed in the ghetto. Some notion of costs and benefits should be used to select the industries and firms to which inducements are offered.

As a general rule, industries which find the central city or the ghetto the least unattractive are already clustered there. Some of these, however, are slow-growing or declining industries, such as food, textiles, and apparel. These businesses are probably not the most desirable, though they should not be dismissed out of hand. Attention should be concentrated on the types of businesses that are already concentrated in the central city and which are stable or expanding nationwide.

Much has been made of the exodus of manufacturing and retail establishments to the suburbs. Wilfred Lewis estimates that between 1959 and 1965, fifteen of the largest central cities lost a total of 195,000 jobs in manufacturing and 174,000 jobs in retail trade to the suburbs.[8] Some argue that the decline in central city manufacturing and trade has run its course and that the balance of technological factors has shifted back toward centralization. They argue that this trend, combined with demands to improve retail facilities in ghettos, will bring added economic activity to central cities. But little can be gained by reasoning on this

[8] Lewis, *Urban Growth*, Table 7.

broad basis. Locational decisions are made by individual firms, some of whom can be induced to locate in the central city with little expense or loss of efficiency. At the same time, it would seem that the shift of retail employment to the suburbs will not likely be reversed. Retail trade is consumer oriented and has followed consumers who are moving to the suburbs. While the population of central cities expanded by 1 percent from 1960 to 1968, the corresponding rise in their suburban rings was 18 percent. The increasing population density of the suburbs, combined with a convenient highway network, has provided the market for specialized products in suburban shopping centers. No longer must consumers journey to the central city to satisfy their needs, and this pattern does not appear likely to change. Furthermore, retail firms face higher costs in the city. Improving the quality of retailing in the ghettos is desirable; but this improvement, with its larger and more efficient units, is likely to replace small businesses and in the process decrease rather than increase retail employment.

Employment in the service sector is an obvious source of jobs for the disadvantaged. This has been the most rapidly expanding sector in the central city, and further expansion is likely because a higher percentage of disadvantaged workers are hired in the services than in manufacturing. Most service employment is public or quasipublic—in federal, state, or local government or in hospitals and educational institutions. Employment opportunities in government, education, and health services should, of course, be increased and improved, and the location of facilities in or near the ghetto should be promoted. But such private service businesses as insurance and finance companies also employ large numbers of low-skilled workers and should be prime candidates for location in the ghetto.

Many types of manufacturing industries could be attracted to the central city or the ghetto and would have a significant potential impact. But there are some obvious limitations. Plants which require ready access to natural resources consume large quantities of water, create severe nuisances or hazards, or require large tracts of land are not suitable for central cities. Even more significant, though often overlooked, is the fact that there are relatively few new, expanding, or relocating manufacturing firms. Between 1958 and 1963, the annual number of new plants was only around 3,500. One-quarter of these were chemical processing plants generally unsuitable for central city location; about two-thirds employed less than twenty people. Actually, many of the 3,500 were firms either located within or moved out of central cities.[9] At a rough estimate, there are fewer than 500 new plants each year which employ more than twenty persons and are suitable for central cities. Competing for these businesses are suburban areas with many relative advantages and rural areas which often have an even greater need for potential jobs than central cities. And considering the fact that between 1958 and 1963 the twenty largest cities suffered a net loss of 850 manufacturing plants, any rapid increase in the number of manufacturing jobs in central cities is unlikely.

Whatever new industry might be attracted to central cities or ghettos, the tradeoff between quality and quantity remains crucial. If the low income of the working poor is considered more critical, then highly capitalized industries which use the unskilled should be sought. On the other hand, if unemployment is the major problem of ghetto residents, job creation must have higher priority and labor-intensive industries should be attracted. If job quality is stressed, the quantity will probably suffer. The heavy capital investment required to produce high paying jobs will require more inducement and subsidy than the smaller and less permanent investments of labor-intensive industries. The choices will not be clear-cut, but the goals should be explicitly stated rather than developed by default.

THE LEVEL OF INDUCEMENTS

Neither experience with federal subsidies nor locational theory provide more than a crude estimate of the subsidies needed to

[9] Management and Economics Research, Inc., *Industrial Location as a Factor in Regional Economic Development* (Washington: Government Printing Office, 1967).

60

attract businesses to the central city and the ghetto on a large scale. Federal programs to aid depressed areas have been in effect since 1961, but they have concentrated primarily on rural communities, and this experience is not transferable to central city conditions. The bulk of expenditures made under these programs was for the construction of public facilities, and it is impossible to determine the effect of an improved infrastructure on the location of firms. Low-interest loans were also offered to firms locating in depressed areas, but it is not clear how much they affected locational decisions.

Economic development efforts in the central city have been limited, and it is dangerous to generalize from their experience in predicting the costs of more intensive efforts. Since 1966 the federal government has subsidized a small number of plants to locate in ghetto areas, but the number of additional firms which could be induced to locate in the ghetto, or the elasticity of this supply of relocating firms, is unknown.

As noted earlier, the Labor Department paid subsidies under the guise of reimbursing employers for training the workers. The average payments per job under this effort have been substantially larger than the average paid under JOBS, and the higher costs are presumably an inducement to locate rather than a reimbursement for measurable training costs. Control Data Corporation, for example, was awarded a $1 million training grant for its 110-employee plant in Minneapolis's Northside. Avco Corporation received a $1.1 million grant to open its 220-man Roxbury printing operation and Xerox was given a $446,000 grant for its 100-employee metal stripping plant in Rochester.

Even though these subsidies were almost twice the average $2,800 per employee contract under JOBS, they did not cover the differential costs of locating in the ghetto. CDC president William Norris estimated that its grant would cover only 15 percent of the higher costs of its ghetto operation. These firms were willing to absorb a portion of these costs as an expense of "corporate citizenship," and there may be other firms willing to do this. But the publicity which accompanied these pioneering efforts accounted for much of the commitment. If plants are to be attracted on a large scale, the publicity value will diminish and monetary incentives will have to be increased accordingly.

The specific goal of the Labor Department's grants under the Special Impact Program was to attract businesses to the ghetto. Ten businesses, five in New York and five in Los Angeles, were given an average of $830,000 in fiscal 1969 to locate near ghetto areas. The experience has not been carefully analyzed, but it is apparently as unfavorable as that of the eight 1968 grants mentioned earlier. The 1968 grants were not tied to training programs because the jobs were low-skilled and the firms had traditionally hired disadvantaged workers. The subsidies, amounting to $3,000 per projected employee, or $1.00 for every $6.50 of capital invested, served to induce firms to locate within commuting distance of the ghetto and to hire disadvantaged workers. As mentioned earlier, all but one of the firms located on the outskirts or completely outside the target area. Harder bargaining and better administration might have induced the firms to locate more centrally within the ghetto, but the inducements might also have been raised. Clearly, luring businesses into the ghetto can be an expensive proposition.

Antipoverty funds have been used to support several local development corporations which, among other things, seek to attract new businesses. For instance, Special Impact funds have been used by the Labor Department to finance Restore, the Bedford-Stuyvesant development corporation, which has given some assistance to a few small plants. Local development corporations have neither the resources nor the expertise to attract larger firms, and their help has come only after the decision was made to locate in the ghetto.

Not all firms locating plants or branches in the ghetto seek a federal subsidy. Brown Shoe Company, for example, located a plant in the center of East St. Louis, and it anticipates that this operation will be fully competitive. IBM decided to locate a plant in Bedford-Stuyvesant without government subsidy, despite a projected $500,000 annual loss over several years. IBM President Thomas J. Watson, who was responsible for this decision, was unquestionably influenced by his membership in the Development and Services Corporation, which was concerned with economic development in Bedford-Stuyvesant. Because most location decisions are made by top management, reaching these executives is a key to increasing the number of central city plant locations.

All things considered, federal, corporate, and local development efforts to date have hardly made a dent in the problems of central cities. Government subsidies have been unable to influence many corporations to locate in depressed urban areas; plants that have been attracted are only a handful compared to those established elsewhere by the same corporations. There is a distinct possibility that corporate involvement will extend little further than the opening of these "showcase" plants. For this reason, several large-scale programs for the economic development of central cities have been proposed.

Tax incentives have been proposed to accelerate business locations in depressed urban areas. The proposal (S. 2088, 90th Congress) of the late Senator Robert F. Kennedy is most relevant. Four incentives were to be offered to firms locating or expanding in poverty areas and employing more than fifty workers from poverty areas: (1) a 10 percent tax credit on investment in machinery and equipment; (2) a 7 percent credit on plant construction costs; (3) accelerated amortization; and (4) a special tax credit of 25 percent of the wages and salaries paid to residents of the area.

It was estimated that the measure would save an employer $91,000 in taxes each year on a million-dollar investment. A Department of Commerce-sponsored study attempted to forecast the proposal's impact on specific industries.[10] The study concluded that 52 of the 160 industries studied might take advantage of the

[10] Jack Faucet Associates, *A Preliminary Analysis of the Economic Effects of the Urban Employment Opportunities Development Act*, Report to U.S. Department of Commerce, Economic Development Administration (Washington: August 18, 1967).

bill's tax provisions. Not surprisingly, the industries that would benefit most were already concentrated in central cities: men's and women's apparel, footwear, leather goods, and textile finishing. The study estimated that over a ten-year period the bill's incentives would develop 250,000 jobs in poverty areas, generating annually $770 million in wages, at a cost to the U.S. Treasury of $500 million. These figures are necessarily "guesstimates," but they indicate the high cost of offering tax incentives to firms for locating in central cities. As noted earlier, the goal of 250,000 jobs paying an average annual wage of $3,000 might be less desirable than the creation of fewer jobs with higher pay. There are already labor shortages in many entry-level jobs, and it is questionable whether bringing more low-skilled and low-paying industries to the central cities will have a significant impact on the market for such jobs. More desirable results might be achieved by restructuring the incentives to attract capital-intensive industries, or by offering employers additional tax credits for raising wages and salaries of disadvantaged workers.

The tax incentive approach of the Kennedy bill is attractive because it minimizes the discretionary role of the government and precludes bureaucratic meddling in private decision making. It is assumed that business decisions within the structured tax framework will insure the most efficient allocation of resources compatible with the development of central cities. This may not, however, be the case. Industries and firms in a position to benefit most from the incentives might move to the ghetto with lesser inducements. For instance, the aforementioned study of the Kennedy bill estimated that apparel industry firms would locate in the central city even if the benefits were reduced by a third. Because the incentives are the same for all firms, those who would have settled for less receive windfalls.

If a large-scale program is desired, there is an alternative to the tax incentive approach: direct grants to city economic development departments, existing local development corporations, or development groups working with antipoverty community action agencies (CAAs). Instead of reducing tax revenues, this scheme would allocate money directly to cities on the basis of need. These cities could then compete as economic units for available firms, hopefully bidding for industries that would maximize their relative advantages. Competitive inducements could take different forms in different areas and for different industries, minimizing windfalls and the distortion of normal allocation. While conceptually appealing, the direct grant approach may not work more efficiently than tax incentives. It is not likely that central cities would be able to determine their best competitive advantages or that the federal government could afford politically to allocate funds according to need.

Given the inherent problems and the dearth of theoretical or empirical knowledge about central city economic development, large-scale programs to attract business are of questionable value. What may be preferable is the continuation of present programs and gradual expansion of those that prove themselves. For instance, additional funds could be allocated to OEO for central city development projects and for local development corporations through urban CAAs or other local agencies. Alternatively, the authority and funds of the Economic Development Administration could be expanded to attract business to central cities. Finally, the Labor Department could offer larger "training" grants to firms locating in depressed urban areas. Efforts to date by OEO, EDA, and the Labor Department have been experimental, and this approach should be continued and expanded only after better understanding is achieved about the viability of central city economies and the level of inducements required to lure firms there.

To suggest continuation and gradual expansion of present programs rather than new and massive development efforts is not to deny the very real problems of ghetto areas. Central cities need help, but subsidized economic development can contribute to alleviating the plight of ghettos only if successful.

First, formidable political difficulties militate against singling out specific areas for attention. Federal efforts to aid depressed areas clearly have demonstrated the pressures to expand eligibility and the difficulty of limiting the benefits of the program on the basis of

65

need. The Area Redevelopment Act was originally conceived to help a few dozen economically depressed cities, but within two years over a thousand counties—one of every three in the country—were made eligible to participate. Similarly, programs to develop ghetto entrepreneurship are not likely to receive a disproportionate share of funds for business development. And there is strong opposition to the very concept of promoting minority entrepreneurship. An AFL-CIO statement on minority entrepreneurship denounced it strongly. "Attempts to build separate economic enclaves, with substantial tax subsidies, within specific geographically limited ghetto areas, is apartheid, anti-democratic nonsense."[11]

Second, there are inherent dangers in implementing massive programs based on limited experience and untried theories. The worst consequence of failure is not just the loss of alternative uses for the funds; the inflated promises which may be necessary to initiate any large-scale effort can compound the problems of the ghettos if the promises remain unfulfilled. And once programs have been initiated, it is often difficult to cut them back even if they prove ineffective.

Third, the problems of the central city are to a large degree intractable, and the proposed remedies do not appear likely to reverse the secular economic decline of the largest cities. One leading study of the spatial distribution of economic activity found, for example, that World War II conditions served to reverse long-run trends toward the dispersion of manufacturing to suburbs and smaller cities.[12] Wartime controls and immediacy of defense needs increased employment in or around existing plants which were concentrated in the larger cities. But as soon as the war

[11] Statement by the AFL-CIO Executive Council on Economic Progress of Minorities (Bal Harbour, Fla.: February 21, 1969).

[12] Daniel Creamer, "Changes by Type of Location 1947–1961," Part I in *Changing Location of Manufacturing Employment* (New York: National Industrial Conference Board, 1963). An alternative view is presented by John F. Kain, "The Distribution and Movement of Jobs and Industry," *The Metropolitan Enigma* (Washington: Chamber of Commerce of the United States, 1967), pp. 4–10.

ended and conditions returned to normal, employment dispersal began again at an accelerated rate. No one can measure the extra costs related to the World War II experience, but admittedly expenses were huge and still had no more than a temporary effect.

Finally, alternatives to programs of central city economic development may be preferable. Rather than bringing jobs to people, greater efforts could be made to increase the access of people to jobs by providing more low and moderate cost housing, eliminating housing discrimination, and improving public transportation. Programs that improve mobility are preferable to those that subsidize immobility. It is, after all, the people of central cities who must be helped and not the central cities themselves. In the longer run the residents of the ghetto must be prepared to qualify for the expanding attractive jobs in the central cities.

4

Developing Minority Businesses in the Ghetto

Income and employment among ghetto residents have improved relatively as well as absolutely during recent years. However, the narrowing gap does not extend to business ownership. Blacks and other minority group members concentrated in the nation's ghettos own a disproportionately small share of the nation's business units. Their relative position has declined rather than improved: between 1950 and 1960, the number of black-owned businesses declined from 42,500 to 32,500.[1]

The low income of residents is one explanation for the limited number of ghetto businessmen, but even more serious is racial discrimination. While the poor are less likely than the nonpoor to own business equity, the proportion of nonwhite poor owning equity is only a third of that among poor whites. Given the concentration of blacks in the ghetto and their growing sense of community, it is understandable that low quality service and retail establishments, which hire ghetto residents but are owned and operated by suburban commuters, would eventually lead to rancor and a feeling of exploitation. The imagery of colonial imperialism is deceivingly applicable to ghetto conditions.

[1] Nathan Glazer, "The Missing Bootstrap," *Saturday Review*, August 23, 1969, p. 57.

There are a number of arguments for increasing internal ownership other than the obvious one that it is a sore spot in the Negro
community. Some of these arguments are valid; some are specious.

The claim that ownership is the primary source of power in our
capitalistic society is a vast oversimplification. Few individuals in
the white community own *and control* any large-scale enterprises,
and transferring ownership of small businesses to blacks adds
little to the power of the black community. There is no reason to
expect that stockowner participation would be any greater in a
large black-owned corporation than in a comparable white-owned
corporation.

But ownership, or more exactly management, of new business
units will force whites to deal with blacks on a "businesslike"
basis, requiring the forms of relationship generally considered
appropriate to the business situation. Social theory asserts that
this "equal-status interaction" is the key to true integration.

Other arguments for locally owned enterprises focus on economic impact. It is obvious that the quality of retail and service
establishments in the ghetto is low, and some claim that entrepreneurship programs will lead to improvement. This may be the
case where new and needed businesses are created, though it is
probably less likely to result from mere ownership transfers.

Less persuasive is the assertion that income will markedly improve within the ghetto by ownership transfers because profits
retained in the ghetto will be re-spent, generating further income
for residents. Profits are a small part of sales, and the dependence
of the ghetto economy on "imports" is so pervasive that the incre-
ment in income resulting from ownership would be miniscule. The
multiplier—which measures the total amount of income generated
by each extra dollar flowing into the ghetto—will increase only
slightly if the profit outflow is closed off. Based on data for
Philadelphia, a citywide multiplier of 1.30 would increase to
about 1.33 if all the profits earned on residents' purchases were
added to the income flow. Thus, little income improvement could
flow from ownership transfers.

In the end, the case for black capitalism rests upon two considerations. First, the belief that equal opportunity should exist in all facets of economic life, that minority groups have suffered from discrimination in the past and have been unable to assume their portion of business ownership, and that equal and even compensatory opportunities must be offered to minorities to help them achieve qualitative as well as quantitative equality of capital ownership. Second, whatever the rationality of the decision, increased ownership ranks high in the priorities of the ghetto community. Clearly, jobs are of first priority; but as these have become more readily available and discrimination against upgrading the skills of Negroes has dwindled, the ownership gap has become a gnawing issue.

Reducing the ownership gap among ghetto residents has been promoted under a variety of banners. Such attempts have been labeled "black capitalism," "ghetto economic development," and black, minority, or ghetto entrepreneurship. Three different activities are usually implied by such terms. First, ghetto residents are to be given financial and technical assistance to purchase and operate ghetto businesses now owned by outsiders. This is perhaps the easiest route to follow, especially now that the riots have made outside owners ready to sell their enterprises. Second, ghetto residents are to be trained and financed to start up entirely new businesses. Though more complicated and risky, this venture could hopefully produce some viable businesses with growth potential. Third, larger corporations are to be induced to establish subsidiaries in the ghetto, gradually transferring ownership and operation to local residents. This final and most difficult strategy has perhaps the greatest potential impact.

Though all three types of activities share a common goal of encouraging ghetto entrepreneurship, they differ drastically in the degree and character of local ownership and control. At one end of the spectrum is the conception expressed by President Nixon in a highly publicized campaign address in 1968, "Bridges to Human Dignity."

For a long time, we . . . have been talking about preservation of the private enterprise system, about enlisting private enterprise in the solution of our great social problems, about profits as the great material power of our fantastically productive economy. What many of the black militants now are saying in effect is this: "We believe you, and now we want a chance to apply those same principles in our own communities."

Our reply should not be to reject this request, but to seize upon it . . . and to respond to it.

The ghettos of our cities will be lastingly remade . . . when the people in them have the will, the power, the resources, and the skills to remake them.

This concept of black capitalism envisions equally and perhaps compensatory opportunities for black businessmen in the traditional entrepreneurial mold. It is a far different approach than that expressed by Roy Innis of CORE, who views black capitalism as a form of community ownership.

By black capitalism . . . we mean the acquisition of the instruments of black capitalism, the community-owned means of operating shops. factories, stores and industry. We're not just interested in creating 10 or 15 black capitalists. . . . What we want is a broad black industrialism, based on community action, ownership and management in the hands of blacks, all the blacks in the community.[2]

In practice, more than conceptual differences have deterred development of minority-owned businesses. Because funds have been severely limited, arguments for "total community ownership" are largely fantasy and rhetoric. The goal has been to create as many black businesses as possible given fiscal and manpower constraints.

As for the future, the debate has centered more on the intensity than on the content of entrepreneurship efforts. In his 1968 campaign, President Nixon endorsed the Community Self-Determination Bill, aimed at establishing locally owned community development corporations which, with tax advantages, would be able to take over ownership and operation of ghetto businesses. President Nixon's endorsement was offered despite the

[2] Quoted in Milton Moskowitz, "Where It's At: Black Capitalism," *Business and Society*, December 17, 1968, p. 3.

fact that the bill contained most of Innis' ideas (he was in fact one of its authors). It is obvious now that the program Nixon contemplated was different in orientation and much smaller than anticipated by Innis. The Nixon administration has apparently settled for providing opportunities on a modest scale for members of minority groups to become entrepreneurs.

Whatever the level of efforts, they must rely heavily on the business sector. Business resources can be tapped to provide financial and technical assistance, markets for the products of minority-owned businesses, and the chance to operate and control larger establishments through ownership transfers of ghetto subsidiaries. The various entrepreneurship programs which have been initiated or proposed are basically alternative means of drawing upon, and effectively utilizing, business sector resources.

THE SBA AND OPERATION MAINSTREAM

The Small Business Administration has thus far played the major role in coordinating private sector resources and promoting minority entrepreneurship. Until recently, this effort was largely unilateral. Under its "6 x 6" program ($6,000 loan for six years), prior to the enactment of the Economic Opportunity Act of 1964, and under its Economic Opportunity Loan (EOL) program since then, it has supplied relatively small and risky loans and some technical assistance to low-income businessmen, with minority group members receiving more than their share of the loans. In fiscal 1968, 40 percent of EOL money (1,200 loans) went to Negroes and other minority groups, constituting three of every four loans to minorities under all SBA programs. Altogether, 13 percent of all SBA loans and less than 5 percent by amount went to minorities.

Under the leadership of former Administrator Howard Samuels, SBA set out to increase the proportion of its loans going to minorities. Given the name Project Own, this effort set as its goal the annual formation of 20,000 minority businesses. This was to be achieved in part by increasing the number of direct loans and providing intensive counseling by a staff of minority entrepreneurship teams located in all the major cities. But even more important, Project Own sought to tap more effectively the resources of the business sector.

Minority businessmen have traditionally found it hard to obtain financing from private lending institutions. The banking community has shunned minority loans because they are presumably riskier; they are also usually smaller, which results in higher overhead costs. Though the SBA had provided loan guarantees at a minimal fee under its business loan programs, banks had not taken advantage of these to make soft loans; they claimed that guarantees involved too much red tape, and that the loans were too small to be profitable. Only ten banks made SBA-guaranteed loans to minority group members in fiscal 1967.

In order to increase bank participation, SBA streamlined its guarantee procedures and reduced the guarantee fee. Administrator Samuels launched a campaign to educate the nation's banks. This effort was fairly successful, and nearly 200 banks have since made guaranteed loans to Negroes or to members of other minority groups, participating in about two-thirds of SBA loans. Project Own, renamed Operation Mainstream by Hilary Sandoval, Jr., the new SBA administrator, has thus been able to achieve greater leverage from SBA minority entrepreneurship allocations.

Considering past discrimination, the dearth of experienced entrepreneurs from minority groups, and the high mortality rate of small businesses, credit alone is not enough. An effective program requires outreach and substantial managerial assistance. SBA's recent experience indicates that about eighty-five hours of management assistance are needed per minority loan. Whatever the exact figure, the process is costly, and SBA's management assistance and minority-loan development staffs of less than 200 persons are already spread thinly. Operation Mainstream therefore looks to volunteers from the business sector to provide assistance. While *businesses* cannot be expected to participate in such a program without profit incentives, *businessmen* are willing and able to give of their time. SBA sees its role as channeling businessmen's

73

social commitment into specialized assistance to minority entrepreneurs. For instance, it has worked at involving trade associations in promoting Negro entrepreneurs. The Ownership Opportunities Program is illustrative. Under this program, the Menswear Retailers of America provide the technical assistance needed by SBA-funded minority entrepreneurs to open clothing stores. Additionally, manufacturers pledged $20 million worth of extended credit to these new stores. A similar program is being developed with leading oil and tire companies for assisting gas stations and automobile accessory outlets. More visionary plans have been proposed to create leagues of businessmen in every city, coordinated by the SBA, to provide management assistance to minorities. Such efforts have been launched independently in several cities, perhaps the best-known effort being the Interracial Council of Business Opportunity, which has branches in seven cities. But these counseling groups lack central coordination or a single source of funding needed for a full-scale mobilization.

SBA has greatly increased the number of loans and guarantees to minority groups. During fiscal 1969, it made 4,120 loans amounting to $93.6 million, up from 1,676 and $29.9 million, respectively, in fiscal 1968. Despite the significant improvement, the number of SBA loans to groups has leveled off. The Nixon administration has been charged with failure to support the very type of program it endorsed so eloquently in the campaign. It has established an Office of Minority Entrepreneurship in the Department of Commerce, with the vague object of coordinating the many programs promoting minority business ownership. But no new resources have been added to the efforts, and thus far it appears that establishment of the new office is just another substitute for action. Additional appropriations needed by the SBA to expand its operations have not been forthcoming, and the outlook appears rather gloomy for the goals of Mainstream. The Small Business Administration lacks the staff for business counseling on the scale needed by untrained businessmen, and its attempts to enlist businessmen's support have met with limited success. Furthermore, there are many within SBA and elsewhere who

74

balk at the high loss rate on minority loans—approaching 15 percent as compared to 2 percent on normal business loans.

Operation Mainstream is, nevertheless, basically a sound idea. The SBA is more qualified than any other government agency to administer the minority entrepreneurship effort, and it is in an advantageous position to tap the resources of the private sector. Dynamic leadership and financial support will be needed, as would be the case for the efforts of any other agency. The slow pace of loans to minority group members under Operation Mainstream should not denigrate the role of SBA in developing minority businesses.

COMMUNITY DEVELOPMENT CORPORATIONS

Another method of establishing ghetto-owned businesses is through local development corporations. There exist a wide variety of such corporations, some funded privately and others publicly, with different degrees of community control and participation by the business sector. Given the present ghetto demand for self-determination, one useful way to classify existing development corporations is on the basis of their origin and control. This breakdown yields three somewhat overlapping categories.

In the first category are establishment-dominated development organizations. These include the Ford-funded Council for Equal Business Opportunity (CEBO) and the Interracial Council for Business Opportunities. Another highly touted effort is the Rochester Business Opportunity Council (RBOC), a local Chamber of Commerce group supported by the city's leading businesses and financial institutions. RBOC makes direct loans to some applicants, refers others to local banks, and coordinates SBA loans. Its most notable achievement has been the establishment of FIGHTON, the black-owned corporation (mentioned in Chapter 3) that employs about 100 workers and produces electrical transformers and metal stampings for the Xerox Corporation. A Chamber of Commerce appraisal attributes the success of RBOC to business involvement: "The single greatest success factor in the

RBOC equation has undoubtedly been the participation of the business community, including its leading figures, from the very outset. These now have brought their own prestige—and the reputations and resources of their companies—into the effort in a sufficiently massive way to allow RBOC to overcome its problems as they come along."[3]

In evaluating RBOC's problems the report focuses, albeit with rose-colored glasses, on the nature of community relations. While some compromises have been forged, such as in the formation of FIGHTON, the relationship between RBOC and FIGHT, a militant black organization, is strained—with RBOC continuing to exclude FIGHT representatives from its board. Such difficulties are characteristic of establishment-linked organizations.

The second group of development corporations is minority-initiated and -controlled. Since many black leaders are establishment men, control over some organizations in this group may be more a matter of color than of substance. Included in this category are New York's Harlem Commonwealth Council, with which Roy Innis is associated; the Green Power Foundation of Watts, 90 percent owned by Negro businessmen and engineers; the Black Economic Union, formed by Jim Brown of Cleveland football fame; and NEGRO, headed by Dr. Thomas W. Matthew of New York. Another well-publicized undertaking is Reverend Leon Sullivan's 10/36 program, in which 3,000 Philadelphia residents have agreed to invest $10 a month for thirty-six months in a "people's installment stock market plan." These contributions made possible the opening of Progress Plaza, a $2.5 million, sixteen-store shopping center. Sullivan insists that effective programs cannot be superimposed on people. Addressing the New York State Savings Bank Association, he stressed the need for black initiative and control, contrasted with the RBOC approach: "The leadership for developing and carrying out these self-help initiatives must come from the people themselves who live where the problems are. The

---

[3] Chamber of Commerce of the United States, Urban Action Clearing House, *Rochester Business Opportunities Corporation* (Case Study No. 6; Washington: Chamber of Commerce, 1968), pp. 4–5.

people must believe and know that the programs to help themselves belong to them, and the successes as well as the failures will be theirs, too."[4]

The third category is distinguished by shared leadership between blacks and establishment men. This group includes Pittsburgh's Business and Job Development Corporation, which has worked closely with Westinghouse Electric Corporation in opening a subsidiary; the Greater Philadelphia Enterprises Development Corporation funded by EDA and SBA; and the Bedford-Stuyvesant development efforts.

In Bedford-Stuyvesant there are two sister corporations. The Bedford-Stuyvesant Restoration Corporation, composed of local representatives, initiates and directs all projects. The Development and Services Corporation, made up of establishment types such as Senator Jacob K. Javits and IBM's Thomas J. Watson, is responsible for bringing in the needed resources. In operation since June 1967, the two corporations claimed twenty-seven new businesses, which had an employment potential of 1,268 by the end of 1968. This claim must be tempered by the fact that five firms with 911 potential employees received no funds or other tangible assistance from the development corporations. The other twenty-two firms were given financial and technical assistance for development and operation. The average direct funding amounted to $35,-000 per firm, while total management assistance costs were about $7,000 per business. Thus, close to $1 million was required to develop twenty-two firms whose average potential is sixteen employees. Even with high initial costs, success is not guaranteed and additional subsidies may be required to train the employees and keep the new businesses in operation.

The degree of community control in the local development corporation does much to determine the type and amount of assistance from the business sector. As a general rule, white dominated corporations are concerned more with business aspects of entrepreneurship than community ownership. They concentrate

[4] Quoted in James Kilpatrick, "OIC's Sullivan, an Apostle of Black Capitalism," *Washington Star*, November 21, 1968.

on developing more traditional types of enterprises with proven and guaranteed markets. Community-dominated corporations are more apt to undertake riskier operations that are visible and potentially beneficial to the whole community. The optimal arrangement may be a dual corporation, as in Bedford-Stuyvesant, which allows for the internal resolution of conflicts between the business sector and the ghetto community. However, businessmen's involvement in such corporations remains voluntary, and any commitment of corporate resources is an act of noblesse oblige. Existing development corporations have lacked the resources to induce large-scale business participation.

Preferred tax treatment has been suggested as one means of increasing the power of local development groups. An example is the Community Self-Determination Bill, introduced in the 90th Congress with broad bipartisan support (which virtually disappeared by the 91st Congress) to create a new locally controlled institution, the Community Development Corporation (CDC). Though CDC would perform welfare and service functions, it is basically an economic institution. Voting stock would be sold at $5 per share or an equivalent amount of "sweat equity," with each member receiving one vote regardless of his holdings. The initial capital would be matched by a federal grant, and further funds would be raised through the public sale of bonds by Community Development Banks, whose voting stock would be wholly owned by CDC.

Preferred tax treatment would enable CDCs to develop their economic endeavors. Under the proposed plan, CDCs would purchase local businesses as well as make loans to them. Ownership is encouraged since a CDC and its subsidiaries would pay only 22 percent on income under $25,000 and 48 percent on income over this amount—compared with 28 and 54 percent (including surtax) paid by other corporations. Dividends paid to a CDC by its subsidiaries would also be tax free.

Even more significant, the proposal would offer special tax concessions to private firms entering into "turnkey" agreements with CDC. Under such agreements, corporations would establish plants, provide training for CDC personnel, and eventually turn over ownership and management of the facility to CDC. In return, the firm would be granted several tax incentives, including accelerated amortization on its turnkey plants and a 10 percent deduction for wages paid to CDC members.

Debate surrounding the Community Self-Determination Bill raised several points that bear repeating. First, ghetto communities often resent acts of "conscience-salving" by the large corporations. Though business participation is required, the ghetto residents' desires to control a "piece of the action" through local development corporations or other machinery should not be ignored. Second, few firms locating in the ghetto are also willing to sell their shares if the businesses prove profitable. And where stock has been offered, as in the case of EG&G Roxbury, workers do not seem very interested in exercising their options. Third, developing entrepreneurship is a difficult task. To saddle such efforts with other social goals possibly erects insurmountable barriers to success. The Community Self-Determination Bill assumes that extensive service and welfare functions can be financed from the profits of CDC enterprises, freeing the community from dependence on the federal role and from control by the establishment. But the firms that would be acquired would for the most part be small or marginal, and their chances for growth and profitability under any management would be limited.

The Potential of Minority Entrepreneurship

Minority entrepreneurship programs have inherent limitations. Most immediate are the manpower constraints. In 1966 there were less than 15,000 black proprietors and managers,[5] and in 1967 the federal government employed only 4,700 Negroes who had

---

[5] U.S. Equal Employment Opportunity Commission, *Job Patterns for Minorities and Women in Private Industry, 1966* (Equal Employment Opportunity Report No. 1; Washington: Government Printing Office, 1968), p. 10.

annual salaries in excess of $12,000.[6] Though this group has increased, and though it does not include the complete universe of potential black businessmen, a shortage clearly exists. This constitutes an immediate constraint on any large-scale program of ownership transfer, whatever arrangements are made to carry out such a program. Black companies would have to compete for black talent and the demand already greatly exceeds the supply. And the chances of blacks learning managerial skills en masse are very small. Moreover, a persuasive case can be made against channeling too great a proportion of emerging Negro executive and administrative capability into running business enterprises. There are other and possibly more pressing needs for their talents.

It is not true that, if funds were more readily available, black entrepreneurs would suddenly emerge. The talented manpower needed to provide expanded technical assistance is not presently available, and it would take years of development to expand the supply. One indication of these shortages is the increasing failure rate in business loans which have come with expanded efforts. Growth of minority loans in the EOL program from 1,200 in fiscal 1968 to 1,800 in fiscal 1969 increased the failure rate from under 5 percent to more than 10 percent. Unless significant losses are accepted, the pace of minority entrepreneurship cannot be greatly accelerated.

But even if Negroes were to achieve equality of ownership, and even if their businesses were as profitable as others, the aggregate effect would not be large. Profits are only a small part of total income. An increase in wages and salaries of 2 percent would have more effect on the total income of the average Negro than a 100 percent increase in the profits he presently receives. Because the average income of blacks is less than two-thirds that of whites, and because wages and salaries form such an overwhelming portion of this income, achieving equality in employment is clearly a higher priority than ownership transfers or entrepreneurial development.

[6] U.S. Civil Service Commission, *Study of Minority Group Employment in the Federal Government* (Washington: U.S. Civil Service Commission, 1967), p. 5.

5

Economic Opportunity in the Ghetto: A Perspective

This study has focused upon three types of programs: those which would open existing jobs to ghetto residents; those which would develop new jobs in or near the ghetto; and those which would promote business ownership by minority group members. What relative emphasis should be given to each of these efforts?

Entrepreneurship programs have the least potential for improving conditions in the ghetto. Even if ownership transfers were accomplished, little additional income would flow into the ghetto because profits are a small part of total income. There are also inherent limitations to developing large-scale entrepreneurship efforts in ghettos, for business opportunities and qualified potential entrepreneurs are in short supply. While ownership opportunities for minorities can and should be expanded, the pace cannot be increased much beyond the present rate without drastically raising costs and failure rates. Enterprising members of minority groups should have the same chance to succeed or fail at the American dream of self-employment as anyone else, and they should face no more risks than those encountered by the majority. However, the payoff is in individual opportunity and it should not be approached as a sufficient answer to the ghetto's problems. The expense of eliminating the "ownership gap" in the foreseeable future does not appear justified by the projected results—though admittedly the psychological impact of minority ownership on ghetto residents should not be ignored, even if it is difficult to assess.

Economic development efforts have more potential, but vastly expanded resources are needed for significant results. Piecemeal efforts tend to be frittered away with few measurable benefits. Experience has shown that the costs of operating in the ghetto can be formidable, and that as a result large businesses are extremely reluctant to locate there. However, a large-scale program could create growth areas in the ghetto so that fewer incentives would be needed to attract firms later on. Certainly many of the present myths and uncertainties concerning ghetto operation could be dispelled. Nonetheless, the potential benefits do not seem to warrant the massive commitment of resources that would be required for a national reverse flow of business from the suburbs to the central city. Despite many inherent difficulties, moving people is cheaper than moving businesses, and in any event the residential ghetto areas have little room for industrial expansion without dislocation or overcrowding.

The most viable of the three immediate strategies is increased access to existing jobs within or in reach of the central city. One means is direct incentives to private employers to hire and train ghetto residents. Despite its current difficulties, the approach is not without promise, though expansion beyond presently limited participation would undoubtedly be costly. Where exhortation and direct incentives have broken down racial discrimination and educational barriers, the costs have not been prohibitive, and employers could be induced to revise their hiring standards either in response to riots or government subsidies or both. But where the disadvantaged are excluded because more qualified workers are available or because they are demonstrably more expensive to hire and train, much larger incentives are required. Program expansion would necessitate more attractive incentives, and the decreased momentum of the JOBS program may indicate that this point has already been reached. The coupling of public institutional skill training and basic education with guaranteed but privately supplied jobs (an approach once tried and abandoned because of the inability of two bureaucracies to cooperate) could expand the JOBS concept into smaller business firms.

The conclusion then seems to be that none of the three strategies should be drastically expanded. All may be justified on the present scale, but only the employment incentives approach might be beneficially expanded at the present time—provided the apparent softening of the labor market does not progress too far. Though each of these three strategies can offer marginal improvements, none of them nor all three together can have a major impact on the future economic development of central cities and improvement of economic conditions for ghetto residents. The challenge to the combined resources of the government and business remains to alleviate the economic problems of minority groups.

The three strategies share an underlying assumption that the combination of federal incentives and corporate citizenship would unleash a flood of private sector resources and know-how into the ghetto. Closely related is the idea, so dear to the hearts of businessmen, that the government is unable to "go it alone."

Experience to date with urban partnership programs has shown that attempts to alter market processes can have little more than a marginal impact. Businessmen can be induced to work for socially desirable ends, but only when these ends do not endanger the profitability of their businesses. Not only must these costs be subsidized, but incentives must be given for doing extraordinary things which involve uncertainty, risk, and a large chance of failure. The costs of luring a firm to the ghetto are more than the higher operating costs. Clearly, it is expensive to swim against economic currents, whether fostering locations in an unattractive business environment or promoting the hiring and training of poorly qualified workers. The resulting costs may mount geometrically with the expansion of the program, and the distortions in the market place may have additional serious side effects.

The costs involved do not negate the desirability of attacking the economic problems of central cities, provided the goal is assigned higher priority than competing pressing needs. If the potential of government-business partnership is limited, other tactics can be developed to achieve the goal of rehabilitating ghetto areas and helping their residents to improve their economic conditions.

Obviously the issues admit no clear-cut answers. To the people trapped in central city ghettos, the problems are real and tragic, though objectively perhaps not as critical as the riots and militant rhetoric might imply. The claim of pervasive sickness in our cities is an exaggeration. The crisis lies partly in the relationship between progress and expectations. Central city problems have always looked serious when viewed statistically. There are large numbers of poor persons, large numbers of workers employed in low-paying jobs, and large numbers of unemployed. But this is because the disadvantaged have traditionally been drawn to the central city as a source of opportunity. In the past, many have found the city a major mechanism of upward mobility. Despite the assertions that the mechanism does not work for Negro immigrants, evidence indicates that the central city still serves as a ladder for the disadvantaged. If it did not, the pace of rural migration would have slowed down. While many continue to live in deprivation in the city, even more have undoubtedly used it as an exit from poverty.

The only real solution to the problems of the disadvantaged is to eliminate their causes. Discrimination in all forms must be ended. Equally important, individual handicaps must be overcome. For ghetto residents this means improved housing, improved education, and improved preparation for employment. Programs to change the economic environment of the ghetto resident should also have a short-run focus, providing employment opportunities until individuals can gain the skills needed to compete in the labor market and the access to exercise their competitive abilities. Ghettos will only be eliminated when their residents become qualified and are given the opportunity to compete and suceed in the mainstream economy.